Pfeiffer Linkage Incorporated

Linkage Inc.'s Best Practices for Succession Planning

Case Studies, Research, Models, Tools

BICENTENNIAL
1807
WILEY
2007
BICENTENNIAL

John Wiley & Sons, Inc.

Published by Pfeiffer
A Wiley Imprint
989 Market Street
San Francisco, CA 94103-1741
www.pfeiffer.com

Linkage, Inc.
One Forbes Road
Lexington, MA 02421
781.862.3157; Fax 781.860.5138
www.linkageinc.com
www.linkageinc.com/ler

Readers should be aware that Internet Web sites offered as citations and/or sources for further information may have changed or disappeared between the time this was written and when it is read.

Pfeiffer books and products are available through most bookstores. To contact Pfeiffer directly call our Customer Care Department within the U.S. at 800-274-4434, outside the U.S. at 317-572-3985, or fax 317-572-4002, ,or visit www.pfeiffer.com.

Pfeiffer also publishes its books in a variety of electronic formats. Some content that appears in print may not be available in electronic books.

Library of Congress Cataloging-in-Publication Data

Linkage Inc.'s best practices for succession planning: case studies, research, models, tools / edited by Mark R. Sobol ... [et al.].—1st ed.
 p. cm.
 ISBN-13: 978-0-7879-8579-0 (alk. paper)
 1. Executive succession—Planning. 2. Business planning. 3. Leadership. I. Sobol, Mark R. (Mark Robert)
 HD38.2.B484 2007
 658.4′01—dc22

                                                                                2007005806

Printed in the United States of America
FIRST EDITION
HB Printing   10 9 8 7 6 5 4 3 2

Contents

Tables, Figures, and Exhibits

Tables

Figures

Exhibits

Acknowledgments

Linkage, Inc., would like to recognize the following outside individuals for their contributions to *Best Practices for Succession Planning: Case Studies, Tools, Models, Research:*

Dale Buss	Jason Pelopida
Janice Duis	Harriet Phillips
Marilyn Figlar	Rob Tucker
Leigh Fountain	Dennis Zeleny
Rachael Lai	Greg Zlevor
Valerie Most	James White
John Murabito	Josef Bataona

We would also like to recognize and thank the following Linkage employees and partners for their valuable time and contributions to this book:

Greg Dracos	Madeline Tarquinio
Desley Khew	Tracy McLaughlin
Sam Lam	Justin Bourke
Ellen Rosenberg	Stacy Thayer

Preface

Our research indicates that one of the top challenges facing today's leading organizations is how to implement an effective succession planning system. Succession planning and the identification and development of top talent are essential for any organization looking to gain competitive advantage. Most organizations recognize the need for succession planning but are unable to follow through on creating a system that will bring long-term results. Effective succession planning enables organizations to exert much more rigor when examining leadership competencies and determining the steps necessary to close identified leadership gaps.

This book combines real-life, pragmatic case studies with hands-on work and advice in the area of succession planning. It profiles what top organizations are doing by way of succession planning and talent development. It includes a new methodology for succession, progression, and development; practical case studies; innovative tools; and a comprehensive Resource Guide.

This publication is intended to be enjoyable and readable for everyone; however, the academic nature of the writing and abundance of raw data tend to preference some specific audiences. Among those who should consider this reading are chief human resource (HR) executives, heads of leadership development, human resource generalists, consultants of succession, and graduate school students.

This book will enable organizations to:

- Identify, develop, and retain top talent
- Assess future roles

- Integrate succession planning with other business and HR models in the organization
- Analyze bench strength
- Design the system
- Implement the plan
- Measure results

Organization of the Book

Best Practices for Succession Planning is divided into four parts, each including individual chapters for easy reference.

Part One: Introduction to Succession Planning

This first part of the book is an introduction to the overall concept of succession planning. It is included to answer questions such as, What is succession planning? How important is it for a successful business? And, how is it used?

Following this conceptual debate is an introduction into the business practices and theories of Linkage, Inc. This includes in-depth descriptions and graphical tools regarding management of high-potential employees, assessment of capability gaps, filling of organizational gaps, leadership development, and employee profiling. In addition to this we have included comprehensive tools to help further the learning process. Among these are question-and-answer sections and a seven-step process to effective succession management.

Part Two: Best Practices in Succession Planning

This part, including Chapters Three to Nine, compromises the meat of the book. Thanks to the contributions of Bright Horizons, CIGNA, AlliedSignal, Lockheed Martin, Merrill Lynch, Ralston Purina Petcare Company, and Unilever, we have compiled a list of best-practice case studies to provide real examples for the reader. These chapters are divided into sections, with subheadings for easy access. Each chapter begins with an introduction to the case study;

this includes an overview of the unique conflict facing the organization, a brief intro to the business itself, a description of what the reader can expect to learn, and an organizational abstract of the chapter. Next is the case study itself; these describe conflicts and business cases to explain the need for succession management for each company, specific looks into the processes used by each business, and description of tangible results. The final part of each chapter is a section entitled "Lessons Learned," briefly summing up the main points of each case study.

Part Three: Succession Planning Toolkit

There is no singular succession strategy that works for all firms and all industries. To be successful a firm needs a plan that meets its individual business needs. The purpose of Part Three, the toolkit, is to provide tools and models that can be used to obtain a generic understanding of succession without a focus on industry-specific examples. This allows the reader to learn the information in a way that is conducive to adaptation, making it conform to his or her specific business culture.

The toolkit part of the book revolves around a specific model entitled "Best-Practice Succession Management Cycle." This model divides succession management into three phases: assessment, development, and evaluation. Using this format, we have included a number of models and assessments for each of the phases, allowing the reader to skip to those areas in which more practice or more learning is needed.

Part Four: Resource Guide

The Resource Guide is meant to organize all study material into a comprehensive outline, making it easy for the reader to navigate through the information used for this publication. Thus, it provides access to a bounty of material for those readers who wish to do their own research in the area and create succession systems on their own. The Resource Guide is organized by type of resource, including books, articles, Web sites, multimedia, and more.

About the Editors

Mark R. Sobol

Mark R. Sobol has gained international recognition through his work with executives and boards of global science and engineering organizations. He is an integral part of numerous initiatives around the world helping client organizations make the big decisions on strategy and leadership that must be designed and turned into action for lasting impact.

His work spans more than twenty-five years of consulting and coaching leaders in multicultural environments in more than forty countries in North and South America, the Caribbean, United Kingdom, Europe, and Asia.

Mark is a member of the faculty of the Global Institute for Leadership Development and the founding principal of Leadership Strategies International, Inc. He is also a member of the advisory panel of the Worldwide Association of Business Coaches.

Publications

Coeditor of *Best Practices in Leading the Global Workforce* (Jossey-Bass, November, 2005).

Coauthor of *The Visionary Leader* (1992) and its final edition: *The Mission Driven Organization*, published by Prima, an imprint of Random House (1999).

Contributing author in *The Handbook of Online Learning: Innovations in High Education and Corporate Training* (Sage, 2004).

Phil Harkins

Phil Harkins is president, CEO, and chairman of the board of directors of Linkage, Inc., the company that he founded in 1988.

Phil is an internationally known expert in the fields of organizational development, leadership, communications, and executive coaching. His clients have included senior executives and teams at Prudential, Kraft, Ralston Purina, Morgan Stanley, American Express, Intel, Microsoft, NASA, Xerox, Cendant, McKesson, US Steel, and numerous other Fortune 500 companies worldwide. All told, Phil has worked with leaders, leadership teams, and boards in more than twenty-five countries located in Asia, North America, South America, Europe, and the Middle East. In addition, along with leadership expert and Linkage board member Warren Bennis, Phil is co-chair of The Global Institute for Leadership Development, which has trained and developed more than 4,000 leaders from around the world.

Phil has authored and edited several books, including *Everybody Wins: The Story and Lessons behind RE/MAX, the World's Largest Real Estate Company* (John Wiley & Sons, 2004); *The Art and Practice of Leadership Coaching* (John Wiley & Sons, 2004); and *Powerful Conversations: How High-Impact Leaders Communicate* (McGraw-Hill, 1999). Phil speaks frequently on these and other topics at public and in-house conferences, seminars, and programs around the globe. Since 1995, he has spoken at more than 400 such events.

Prior to founding Linkage in 1988, Phil held senior management positions at Keane, Inc., and Raytheon (both in the United States and abroad). He also served on the faculty and as a senior administrator at Boston University. He currently serves as a member of the Board of Directors for Keane, Inc.

Phil is a graduate of Merrimack College and received three advanced degrees from Harvard University. He resides in Concord, Massachusetts.

Terence P. Conley

Terry Conley is chief administrative officer of Travelport, formerly Cendant Travel Distribution Services.

Prior to this role, Terry was executive vice president of human resources and corporate services for Cendant Corporation. Cendant was primarily a provider of residential real estate and travel services operating in over 100 countries and generating $18 billion in revenue.

With over 20 years of human resources experience, Terry oversaw global HR, facilities management, corporate real estate, events marketing and security functions throughout the enterprise. Under Terry's leadership, his team launched a company-wide "Employer of Choice" initiative to over 90,000 Cendant employees, significantly increasing Cendant's employee engagement and organizational capability.

Terry has extensive experience in both strategic and operational human resource management with multiple industries including retail, manufacturing, restaurant, financial services, real estate, travel and consumer products.

Prior to joining Cendant, Terry spent nearly 10 years with the PepsiCo organization with HR leadership assignments in corporate and all their subsidiaries. His last position was vice president of human resources at The Pepsi-Cola Company. In this role, Terry culminated his career by leading the HR aspects of the formation of independent bottling entities as a result of the break-up of the Pepsi-Cola sales and distribution organization. Prior to this role, Terry was director of human resources with PepsiCo's Frito Lay division, director of human resources for PepsiCo corporate and director of human resources with PepsiCo's KFC unit. Previously, Terry served in various HR capacities with RH Macy & Company.

Terry received his Bachelor of Science degree in management and marketing from New York University.

Part One

INTRODUCTION TO SUCCESSION PLANNING

1

A NEW METHODOLOGY

Succession, Progression, and Development

Our goal in this chapter is to identify the complexities of succession management so that each individual who picks up this book can walk away with a clear sense of how to succeed when developing a succession plan. To do this we have organized the following sections of the chapter to follow a gradual process of solving the challenges that are most frequently responsible for turning brilliant ideas into smoldering ruin. This common misconception regarding succession is simple yet very difficult to avoid: succession is not a single process. It's all too easy to satisfy an organization's need for talent by devising a linear plan, recruiting, and setting up a bench system of qualified leaders. This, however, is not sufficient. The key to succession, which too many overlook, is the concept of *sustainability*. The successful strategy must not only allow for assessment and recruitment, but also development, progression, discussion, evaluation, and oftentimes the adoption of an entirely new corporate culture. Rather than planning in a straight line, the talented leader must create a repeating cycle that will ensure success now and in the future.

The chapter begins with an introduction to the "Age-Old Debate," in essence proving the need for a multifaceted organizational ruling body. The *power of four* theory is then introduced, showing the logic behind our reasoning and gradually leading up to the discussion of the proven solution, the Succession/Progression/ Development (SPD) system. This system is then broken down into pieces that can be mixed and matched, rearranged to conform to an infinite variety of industries, corporate cultures, and business models. To conclude the chapter we present a list of common questions and concerns relating to the implementation of the SPD program, as well as various tools and models to add an element of perception to the learning process.

Chapter Outline

The Age-Old Debate
The Power of Four Theory
The Jack Welch Example
Conclusions Drawn

The Succession Planning Process

The Ten Questions and Answers That Explain SPD for the Board

The Age-Old Debate

Some people say high-impact organizations are a function of leaders like Jack Welch; then success—that is, high impact—happens. Other equally fervent arguments state that high-impact success is dependent on building great teams embedded in a strong culture, supported by healthy values, not single leaders. This "great leader" versus "great organization" argument can be referred to as "the age-old debate." One question remains: Which is right?

Our conclusion points to a possible solution to and explanation for this controversy, as we are sure that both sides of this argument hold water. For certain, great organizations require teams of focused and aligned workers who in aggregate are able to execute against a plan to drive the strategy. At the same time, however, these organizations need strong leaders who are passionate. These passionate leaders create what we call the *power of four*; they drive energy down into the organization by creating multiple levels of passionate leadership.

On the one hand this seems obvious. Strong leaders and strong organizations are by-products of each other. On the other hand, it is the chicken and the egg—which comes first? Does it matter? Our experience in this study makes us confident in saying that organizations need both: strong leadership *and* an integrated system for succession, progression, and development. In fact, each is highly dependent upon the other. We also believe a strong leader makes a difference. How does this happen in real time?

Let us propose this axiom: *High-performing organizations are not accidental occurrences*. Boards of directors know this best. They spend a significant amount of board time providing oversight, ensuring that the right top leaders are in the right place. Today more and more board directors are aware of the power of four, although they obviously don't call it that. Instead, directors whom we have interviewed have said that "we need to have the right leadership with the right strategy, structure, and values." What are boards most worried about then? We asked a number of board chairs this question: "What keeps you up at night?" The common answer: "Leadership."

What does this all mean and where does it lead us? It is certain that one leader cannot do it alone. Therefore "the great man" argument must be wrong. The great stories of high-performing organizations we have researched are rich in that they have many leaders intricately woven around strategy, execution, systems, and growth. We also found this to be true in our prior research (published in a book called *Everybody Wins* [2004]), where we studied organizations that were consistently successful over long periods of time (thirty years). Our earlier study revealed that the most highly successful, high-performing, high-impact organizations all displayed the same persistence and focus on succession, supported by providing progression and development opportunities for their high-potential leaders (HIPOs). This important strategy, putting emphasis on the individual through potential-based prioritization and established progression objectives, is discussed later in the chapter.

The Power of Four Theory

According to the arguments just mentioned, high-impact organizations cannot focus on one leader alone; instead they must concentrate on the concept of *leadership*. What does this mean for succession, progression, and development? Simply put, the best organizations we could find are vigilant in creating layers of leadership. This substantiates a pattern of organizational behavior for highly successful businesses that we call the *power of four theory*. An example of this might be the heads of HR, marketing, public relations, and finance. This means that when there are four powerfully intertwined leaders at the top of an organization, they have the ability to create true passionate champions. It is important here to summarize to make sure that the reader understands the significance of this point, for we believe that there is substantial power in creating layers of passionate champions.

The concept of the *passionate champion* is a simple one. There are three parts: (1) a passionate champion is someone who is completely ardent and who wants the result more than his or her boss does; (2) the passionate champion is more capable of delivering results (has more specific core competencies: skills, knowledge, and abilities) than the boss; and (3) the passionate champion makes it happen *somehow*—delivering consistently against all odds.

This concept of the passionate champion is one that is of utmost importance to any business. We believe that there is a strong relationship between the concept of the power of four—having four passionate champions at the top two levels of organizations— and creating high-performing businesses. The research conducted for the *Everybody Wins* project reinforces our convictions that the best organizations in the world spend significant amounts of time planning succession, organizing progression discussions, and ensuring that there are development plans in place for those who are on succession charts.

The following example is meant to elaborate on our premise regarding the need for high-performance teams at the top of the organization. It is important to note that there is another lesson that can be learned here regarding the role of the chief executive officer (CEO) in the succession process. Although it is not recommended to operate in an organizational monarchy, it is essential to have a qualified CEO who recognizes the need for managing internal talent. As the example shows, succession is a businesswide ordeal, but the process of selling and approving a strategy will not leave the ground without the consent and enthusiasm of a qualified CEO.

The Jack Welch Example

Suppose we were to take Jack Welch out of retirement and place him into a troubled company like General Motors. Would he make a difference? The great leader proponents would say, "Absolutely." Those who believe that culture, values, and other ingredients result in teams of leaders who make a difference would say, "No." We recently tried this at a YPO meeting of fifteen CEOs. All but two said that Jack Welch would make a difference. The group was then asked if they would buy General Motors stock. All but one said yes. In response to their feedback, the groups were asked to elaborate on how much the stock would increase. The range was from 10 to 25 percent on Day 1. Would this really happen? Some top-ranked analysts were called and were asked the same question. The overall consensus was conclusive; General Motors stock was anticipated to grow by a significant amount.

This was intriguing, because Jack Welch, in the past thirty years, has only infrequently driven any automobile, nevermind run the largest automobile company in the world. The fact is Jack Welch mostly sits in the back seat. He has never designed a new model for a car, written a business plan for a car company, or worked in a car dealership. We have been told by those who know him that he hasn't even been to that many dealerships. So the next rational question in this case would be, "What would he do that would increase the value of this company?" To answer this question, we consulted some individuals who had been in senior manager roles at General Electric (GE). Here's a summary of what they said: Welch would redefine the strategy, organize work teams to execute against the strategy, create systems to support it, and look for new opportunities to grow the business. In an attempt to elicit more information, the managers were then asked another question: "What would he do first?" The general consensus was simple: "He would assess the talent and he'd get the right top people in the right jobs. These would be leaders he could count on." In these discussions it was learned that what Jack Welch would *really* do is align the organization around a strategy and aim the top leaders at executing against the strategy. He would do this two or three levels down into the organization, and then he would build organizational backup talent. It was also learned that he would move people around, giving them different responsibility until the organization got it right. Where leaders had holes in their competency profiles, he would find ways to get them up to speed as quickly as possible, and all agreed he would have a backup two deep for every key job. It would be a transparent system. Roles would be clear, people would be held accountable, and, most important, he would make the *hard call*. He would not mistake competence for loyalty, and if he didn't see a passioate champion in a key role he would move the next person up.

What do we conclude from this? Does this support the great leader theory or the leadership theory (more than one leader is required to make a difference)? We think it supports both. Perhaps the single most important thing that Jack Welch did at GE is build an integrated system of succession, progression, and development. He became a great leader because he knew that it took more than one person to accomplish his company's goals. Everyone at GE knew that to survive at the top they had to be a passionate champion. Failure results in a succession decision or a rotation decision. It's not only succession on a chart that works; it's moving people into various positions in order to get it right and having the wherewithal to develop people two levels down to make sure the organization has a certain future.

The reason that succession must be connected to progression is that there is no way to get it right all the time. Succession is not a perfect science. There are a lot of moving parts. In fact, succession requires picking the right person, picking the right time, and picking the right place. Sometimes people are ready and sometimes they aren't; human factors are not always predictable. That is why succession, progression, and development must become an ongoing system as opposed to a single process. Organizations that do their succession planning once per year lose the opportunity to constantly stay in tune with the shifting readiness as well as the wants and needs of all those individuals on organizational charts. For this reason, we recommend that succession planning happen in such a way that it is followed by succession, progression, and development dialogue with all those who appear on organization charts. The results of these dialogues are two important documents. One is an individual development plan (IDP; discussed more fully later in the chapter) and a vulnerability assessment, which measures the risk factor of losing a person who appears on a succession chart (example presented later in the chapter). This vulnerability assessment process is a critical part of succession, progression, and development (SPD) planning, for we believe that turnover is predictable if there is consistent dialogue regarding what people want and need.

Conclusions Drawn

Before we get into the example of a succession, progression, and development system, we will sum up our top ten conclusions about succession, progression, and development:

1. The great leader theory is wrong. High-impact leadership is right.
2. There are great leaders. They are differentiated in that they have the courage to step up and make the hard decisions on succession. They do this best by creating a system around talent management at the top.

3. Succession by itself does very little good if it is the exercise of a once-a-year planning process that is kept in a drawer. Still, it is better than nothing. It forces the organization into a discipline of keeping track of top talent.

4. The difference in high-impact organizations like the ones that we studied in the *Everybody Wins* book is they continually work the succession chart by having dialogue sessions with all those on charts to be sure they know what these individuals need and what they want, as well as what the organization needs from them.

5. From these dialogue sessions come development plans. The best organizations not only know what their next job might be, but they are joined in the plan of providing pathways that include rotations in order for them to get there. Every leader in these organizations has a personalized development plan that is sometimes connected to the performance management system.

6. Some organizations that we consider best in class take it to another level and do risk assessments on succession charts, discussing vulnerability at the board and the executive committee level.

7. The power of four is a way to track organizational soundness. Where organizations have two levels of the power of four, approximately twenty leaders are identified as passionate champions. This creates restful nights for those at the top of organizations.

8. We find that high-performing organizations have someone appointed and accountable for an SPD-type system.

9. Some organizations even take it to the next level, where they accelerate the development of their top leaders, as is the case at McKesson Corporation. We call this *fast tracking*. There they take nothing for granted.

10. On a very practical note, executives lead the board on succession, progression, and development discussions. They don't wait to respond to board directives regarding succession, progression, and development.

The Succession Planning Process

This second part of the chapter presents information, documents, and forms that can be used in the succession planning process. Exhibit 1.1 is a real SPD initiative that can be prototyped and used in organizations. It is set up in such a way to capture the essence of what succession, progression, and development should be, and it also provides action steps that can become a blueprint for implementation.

Figure 1.1 presents three views of SPD: those of the employee, the manager, and senior management or the board. Exhibit 1.2 shows an example of a succession planning book layout. There is no such thing as a latent passionate champion. They are always self-acknowledged fast trackers who best represent the definition of

Exhibit 1.1 Succession Planning Process

1. High-potential employees (HIPOs) are identified and discussed monthly in management meetings.
2. HIPOs have six-month SPD progress discussion with manager and mentor.
   - Review individual development plan (what's happening)
   - Vulnerability assessment (what's new or changing work/life)
3. Executive committee meets twice per year, every six months, on SPD, to plan or review succession and update charts—and discuss changes—as well as IDPs. Specific reviews on "at-risk" HIPOs from vulnerability reports.
4. Board reviews of SPD
   - Board annual review on succession progression development
   - Board semiannual review on succession chart update and vulnerability assessment
   - Board quarterly review of turnover

Figure 1.1 Three Views of SPD (HIPO, Management, Senior Leadership/Board)

HIPO ⟶
Knows where she or he is going and how to get there and feels "cared about" and engaged in the process

- Progression pathway: Sees the steps to advance
- Two development discussions per year: Dialogue, candid, clear, and committed action creates a feeling of trust
- Individual development annual plan: Awareness (self)—assessment/feedback/training/coaching/mentoring

Management ⟶
Knows what is going on and needed by the HIPO and is involved in planning

- Planning progression rotations and opportunities to develop and sees ways to build bench strength
- Two development discussions: Dialogue reveals risk and needs
- Individual development annual plan: Sets up learning master plan; sees the development processes at work and opportunities to advance progression

Senior Leadership/Board ⟶

- Clear view of successors: Sees possibilities for driving strategy
- SPD reports provide line of sight to risk: Intervention
- Sees where development improves retention and oversight to future growth

Exhibit 1.2 The Succession Planning Book Layout

Part I: Succession Plan Charts

- Significant positions are identified and top thirty work profiles completed
- All organization charts for top three levels below CEO
- All positions on organization chart have incumbent and A, B, C, candidates (when one position is vacant—so noted A = ready now; B = six months to two years; C = two to five years)

Figure 1.2   Succession Plan Chart

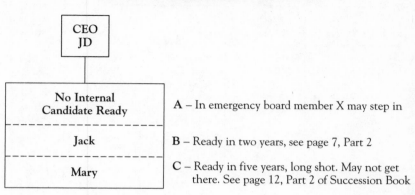

CEO JD

No Internal Candidate Ready	**A** – In emergency board member X may step in
Jack	**B** – Ready in two years, see page 7, Part 2
Mary	**C** – Ready in five years, long shot. May not get there. See page 12, Part 2 of Succession Book

Part II: Succession Plan Notes

Each HIPO has a profile page including:

• Bio and competency profile
• Strengths
• Development needs
• Individual development plan
• Vulnerability (risk) assessment
• Progression path
• Next steps/job

passionate champion presented earlier in this chapter. An example of a succession plan chart is presented as Figure 1.2.

Table 1.1 presents a hypothetical yearly schedule for SPD. Figure 1.3 is a graphical representation of the four phases of SPD: design the system, analyze resources, prepare implementation, and monitor. Figure 1.4 is a flowchart of a possible first year of responsibility for each level of the SPD. Figure 1.5 shows a Learn-Map Pyramid. Exhibit 1.3 presents the vulnerability assessment.

There is no one single SPD process that is right for an organization. The suggestion for using this system is to study the organization's culture and look at how succession is currently being done, then realistically adapting SPD to your organizational climate

Table 1.1 SPD: A Look at a Yearly Schedule (Hypothetical)

	Design System	Analyze Resources	Implement	Monitor	Measure
S U C C E S S I O N	• Identify HIPOs • Define the job profiles	• Review HIPOs • Build succession charts • Review w/board	• Succession dialogue with HIPOs • Complete vulnerability report	• Review trouble spots	• Update charts • Hold second dialogue • Update vulnerability report
P R O G R E S S I O N	• Identify paths and competencies/ experiences required	• Analyze HIPO's experiences • Discuss possible routes for each HIPO short term/ long term	• Prepare pathways for short term/ long term • Career Map—for each HIPO	• Check for possible job rotations • Look for mentor relationships	• Update progression pathways for 2007 • Focus on key HIPOs
D E V E L O P M E N T	• Create possible development alternatives • Gather data on best programs • Pick internal/ external coaches/ mentors	• Prepare company-sponsored programs for HIPOs • Pick the accelerated class: 4–8 fast trackers • Train internal coaches mentors	• Prepare Individual Development Plans (IDPs) • Get approvals for all development • Implement assessment phase	• Check progress on HIPOs • Meet with internal/ external coaches	• Executive review of development and preparation for 2007 • Executive reviews for the fast track
	Q1 '06	Q2 '06	Q3 '06	Q4 '06	Q1 '07

Figure 1.3   Four Stages of SPD

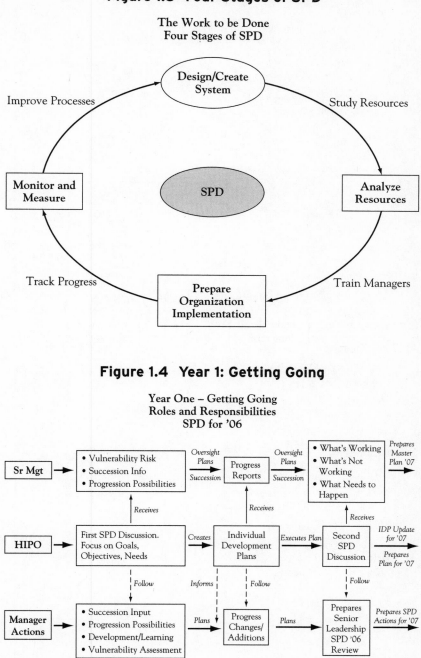

The Work to be Done
Four Stages of SPD

Figure 1.4   Year 1: Getting Going

Year One – Getting Going
Roles and Responsibilities
SPD for '06

Figure 1.5 LearnMap Pyramid

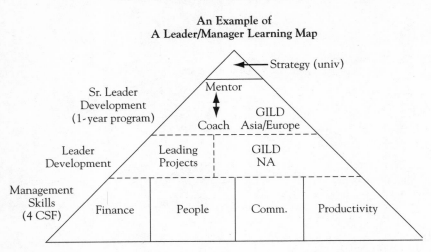

**An Example of
A Leader/Manager Learning Map**

Exhibit 1.3 Vulnerability (At Risk) Analysis

Categories	At Risk	Watch For
1) Comp/Benefits	Yes/No	Learning curve ahead of normal
• More than 10% off market median salary	____	
• Benefits less than competition	____	
2) Position/Title	Yes/No	Peers/friends advance
• Title is not what s/he wants	____	
• Org position is not first choice	____	
3) Work/Life Fit	Yes/No	Changes in family/personal status
• Work hours do not fit life needs	____	
• Location doesn't fit life's schedule	____	

(Continued)

Exhibit 1.3 (*Continued*)

Categories	At Risk	Watch For
4) Boss/Supervisor	Yes/No	Feedback from boss is frequently
• Boss doesn't spend time with her/him	____	critical
• Boss doesn't agree with work habits	____	
5) Team/Environment	Yes/No	Doesn't go to off-hour events
• S/he doesn't have a work friend	____	
• Team doesn't include him/her in activities	____	
6) Learning/Development	Yes/No	No learning opportunities in
• S/he is not learning anything new	____	one year
• There are no opportunities for development	____	

Actions

1. Have a discussion with HIPO—minimum one hour.
2. Check in on the six categories (and two questions).
3. Ask probing questions balancing inquiry with advocacy.
4. Make sure to hit all twelve questions presented on the assessment.
5. At the conclusion, immediately circle yes/no for each category.

    1 = yes = some risk—may stay for one year more

    2 = yes = high risk—may leave within six months

    3 = yes = will leave with a reasonable offer within six months

Note: Managers need to be trained on how to use this tool.

and preparedness. For some organizations, implementation in stages is a better route. Some organizations can digest SPD best over a two- to three-year period. In fact, SPD can backfire if it's implemented too quickly or with an organization that's not ready. In these cases it's better to go for a phased-in implementation.

The Ten Questions and Answers
That Explain SPD for the Board

For additional reference, a collection of "ten questions for the board" is provided following.

1. What is SPD?

SPD stands for succession/progression/development. It is a set of core processes connected together into a seamless system for ensuring that every high-potential employee knows that company leadership, including the board, is focused and invested in their work/life and career. What is different and better about this system is that each core process (succession, progression, and development) is integrated so that high-potential employees (HIPOs) recognize how they can achieve their objectives.

- *Succession* is a formal process whereby the top three tier jobs have clearly defined "backups." Each next-in-line candidate can then be tracked for progression and development. This becomes a visible process for executives and board members. HIPOs also know that they appear on succession charts that spawn discussion on an ongoing (scheduled) basis, allowing them to feel connected to the processes for their own development.

- *Progression* is a tracking process that creates visible pathways for career development. It can be as simple as associate engineer through principal engineer. By having visible pathways, HIPOs can track their career steps and see what bases they need to touch in order to achieve their ultimate objectives. It provides the manager with the visuals to have open discussions that lead to opportunities for rotations, coaching/mentoring, and training.

- *Development* is a more defined process for charting what skills, knowledge, and experiences are required to meet the career path and succession needs for HIPOS. Every HIPO is expected then to have a yearly individual development plan that is reviewed with the manager and is taken into consideration for rotational decisions as well as professional advancement and succession.

2. Why implement SPD now?

The company is at a size and the market conditions are such that attracting and retaining HIPOs is critical to the future of the company. Research through the Corporate Leadership Council points to a worldwide crisis resulting in a war for talent. Companies that manage their succession, progression, and development for HIPOs have higher retention of executive talent. SPD is both an early identification as well as a carefully crafted method to build loyalty. With local market conditions tightening, although cyclical, there is little doubt that the company will continue to be a target for other companies to try to cherry-pick top talent.

3. How does SPD work?

Although backed by an intricate set of processes, SPD is a simple system, particularly as seen by the HIPO. From the HIPO point of view, the individual clearly understands that he or she has been selected as a succession candidate (perhaps even for more than one job). The HIPO also knows that progression, which implies touching a number of bases (that is, jobs along the way), is a requirement for advancement. Becoming more knowledgeable, learning new skills, and overall gaining experience is critical for his or her future. This is all reflected on a yearly individual development plan (IDP). The heart of SPD is in two development discussions per year. The discussion focuses around the HIPO's objectives, and there is agreement on that HIPO's development, including his or her progression. It is in this discussion that the manager is able to reach a clear understanding as to short- and long-term goals and relates all to progression and succession. At the same time, the manager is able to glean important information about that HIPO's work/life and career satisfiers. Each development discussion results in a "sign-off" on the HIPO's IDP. The manager submits for the file a checkup that includes a retention assessment, which identifies risks around six categories of satisfiers.

4. How does the company benefit from SPD?

By using SPD as a system, it keeps the attention on the HIPO front and center. In short, it allows the company to compete for top talent through talent management. The company becomes known not only as a great place to work, but as an organization that has committed time and resources to a strategic and unique program created to ensure the success of the HIPO. Moreover, it is perceived as the company to grow with and be with.

5. Is SPD really about retention?

SPD will help with retention while providing safety and security to the company by ensuring that there is talent in a getting-ready state for every important senior role in the company. When there is turnover, there is opportunity. SPD should help in recruiting and creating a healthy competitive environment for advancement.

6. What does it mean to be a HIPO?

Those who are high-potential employees know that they have been selected and designated for advancement, which requires frequent conversations and a focus on development.

- HIPOs are on a succession chart.
- Each HIPO is on a progression pathway.
- Each HIPO has an IDP that is reviewed yearly.
- HIPOs have two SPD discussions per year, including a vulnerability assessment (see Exhibit 1.2).
- HIPOs progression and development is reviewed by senior management and presented to the board.

7. How does succession planning happen?

Each year at a designated time the succession plan is reviewed by senior management and the board. At that time, the succession plan is studied for vulnerability, that is, specific areas where there is "vacancy" or no immediate candidates ready for key positions within the next two years. Discussion and action plans are put in place. Also at this time, fast trackers are identified. A fast tracker is a HIPO who needs to accelerate his or her development in a special yearlong development process. All IDPs are updated and placed in the succession planning book.

8. How does one become selected for HIPO status and fast track designation?

Senior managers throughout the year continually focus on identifying high-potential employees. This begins with an early identification program at the point of hire and continues through performance reviews and project evaluations. Employees can be designated at any time during the year as a HIPO. It only requires creating an IDP, scheduling a "sit down" to discuss career progression, and beginning to think in terms of how a newly designated HIPO fits into succession.

The objective is to fortify the succession plan by advancing the development of HIPOs who have the capacity to advance quickly and progress at a faster rate.

9. What is a vulnerability assessment?

A proven method for increasing retention of HIPOs is to stay on top of the wants and needs as well as the overall career development of HIPOs. Every HIPO will continually be "checked in" on to ensure that the six proven satisfiers at work (listed in Exhibit 1.2) are reviewed with each HIPO. All managers will be trained on how to have this discussion so it is comfortable and ongoing, showing that the company is truly interested in doing all it can to provide the opportunities at the company that HIPOs are looking for.

Six satisfiers that are proven retention determinants for high potentials (Linkage™):

1. Compensation/Benefits
2. Position/Title

3. Work/Life Fit

4. Boss/Supervisor

5. Team/Environment

6. Learning/Development

10. How is SPD managed?

It does take a fair amount of work to set up SPD. Once the architecture is in place, the system designed, the plan implemented, the initial bench strength analyzed, HIPOs selected, IDPs set in place, it becomes a monitoring and measurement set of tasks. This then becomes a human resource function and a management imperative to monitor. SPD requires a belief, beginning with the board, that succession, progression, and development is a core set of processes and thus a system that is a critical success factor for the company.

2

SEVEN-STEP PROGRAM TO MAXIMIZE YOUR SUCCESSION PLANNING SYSTEM

> The ability to make good decisions regarding
> people remains one of the last reliable sources of
> competitive advantage, since very few organizations
> are very good at it.
>
> —*Peter Drucker*

Why is succession planning a necessity for the success and growth of organizations today? Our research indicates that one of the most critical questions facing leading organizations is how to develop the next generation of leaders. Today's organizations are facing higher demands in a global market. In order to stay afloat and gain competitive advantage, these organizations need to be proactive and prepared for future performance with a "ready-now" workforce. They need to invest in their people through a systematic succession planning system. Despite the growing importance of developing talent, few organizations have taken the necessary steps to make this work or to understand the true meaning of how a succession planning system impacts long-term success and stability.

So, what is *succession planning*? It is a systematic approach to ensuring that an organization has a steady, reliable pipeline of talent that will meet the organization's future needs in leadership and other linchpin roles. With a shortage of talent crippling organizations, why are so many unable to make succession planning work?

The human capital evolution that has occurred over the past fifty years requires companies to change their views of their people. They can no longer view employees as commodities or tools. In today's market, employees are assets. What does this mean? Essentially, it means that companies need to be invested in the welfare of their employees and need to build career paths that will benefit not only the future of the organization but also the future of these individuals. How can your organization build a succession planning system that will stay ahead of trends in today's environment and respond to both the needs of your organization and of your employees?

In Chapter One, we introduced the new concept of SPD, a system that integrates succession, progression, and development. Building on this theme, in this chapter we identify seven steps that are critical components to designing and implementing a successful succession planning program. The best-practice organizations included in this book have relied on these components to create strong programs in their organization. Through their experiences, they present the most up-to-date descriptions of succession planning. They will help organizations build succession pipelines and create a pool of qualified employees who are prepared to accept new leadership roles and drive organizations to reach critical business objectives. The benefits of a systematic succession management system and the SPD methodology are extensive, preventing the high cost of turnover and establishing trust and loyalty from your employees.

The following seven steps are the key ingredient to helping you place the right people in the right jobs at the right time for the right reasons.

1. *Build a development mindset in your organization*. The first step in developing an effective succession planning system begins with a new outlook. The challenge for organizations is how to change their mindsets from viewing employees as a cost to leading, nourishing, and developing human capital as an asset. By choosing to manage people as tangible assets, organizations can be transformed on every level, not just on talent development. This mindset change will help you integrate an SPD model into your organization. It will build the loyalty of employees and help to keep "A" players invested in the future of the organization. Before beginning

a succession planning system, organizations need to take a look at how they view themselves and make the necessary changes to be champions for their employees. Organizations need to adopt the motto that "knowing our product means knowing our people." By building a development mindset, organizations can motivate their employees and help drive performance. Highly motivated workforces will come from a mindset change.

2. *Drive organization alignment both domestically and internationally*. Organizations need to look at the big picture when it comes to succession planning. Chapter One emphasized the theory that "succession by itself does very little good." Drawing on the concept behind the SPD methodology, it becomes clear that in order to be successful, a succession planning system needs to be integrated with the overall business model. This step is the most critical component of your program because if the succession planning program does not support the business, it will ultimately fail. If it does not, organizations need to ask themselves, "Why are we doing it?" Business units think in terms of "If you are not for me, you are against me," so a succession planning program needs to respond to the needs of business. Organizations are like a crew team; everyone needs to row in the same direction. If succession planning is not aligned with the business strategy, organizations will easily miss their talent development objectives and long-term goals.

3. *Inspire a "learning organization."* The best-practice organizations included in this book have been successful at challenging their employees and business units. Before embarking on a succession path they realized the importance of sharing their experiences and learning from the experiences of their employees. In order to be a learning organization, it is important to take the time to document and discuss the lessons learned, both positive and negative. Learning organization have an open mind to doing things a different way. They are responsive to change and reward risk taking. They continually share information and rely on cross-functional teams. It is essential to know the organization and the employees

and learn from them. By establishing a learning organization, the best-practice organizations have been able to stay ahead of trends in the global environment and also have been better able to place their best players in their most critical jobs.

4. *Ensure data-driven decision making.* In the past, succession planning has been viewed as an art, a process that cannot be measured by scientific means. This view of succession planning can be detrimental to an organization's stability. The best-practice organizations profiled in this book have made the necessary shift to replacing the intuition of their succession planning program with science. This shift means that succession planning is driven with the mindset of marketers, economists, and engineers. By using analysis to create change, their succession planning programs have gained credibility. Ensuring data-driven decision making will allow organizations to look at bench analysis and leadership pipelines to determine if they have improved. It will also allow organizations to measure factors such as diversity, progression, and development and incorporate the basics of the SPD methodology.

5. *Segment, align, and develop talent.* Segmenting, aligning, and developing talent is critical to driving operational excellence and organic growth. This component also supports the SPD concept because it emphasizes that succession planning should not be viewed as a single process. In short, *segmenting* involves knowing the strongest performers and recognizing their impact on productivity. *Aligning* talent is ensuring that star performers fill jobs that have the biggest impact on the organization. *Developing* talent can be defined simply as preparing our current and future leaders. Development of top talent has to be considered essential to the organization by executives, senior executives, and line managers.

6. *Continually assess your performance culture.* Why do so few employees actually meet their performance potential? How can organizations enable their employees to perform better? The potential of an organization's employees is a direct reflection of its work setting. These two factors go hand in hand. They are not exclusive.

Continually assessing your performance culture is imperative to a long-term succession planning system. In order to have capability improvements, organizations need to identify the right people in the right jobs at the right time and for the right reasons. Yet, somewhere in this process, organizations lost the focus on performance. They placed people in positions because of their potential but did not measure performance. As a result, people were kept in the wrong jobs and either failed to move up or failed to move on. Organizations need to make sure employees on benchmarks are performers. The best-practice organizations included in this book were able to accomplish this, and as a result, grow their leadership pipelines. Continuing to assess your performance culture involves driving performance, building trust, satisfaction, commitment, retention, and engagement of your employees. These qualities are essential and will empower your employees to go above and beyond the call of duty.

7. *Gain the support and participation of the chief executive officer (CEO) or president in the process.* Once your succession planning system is aligned with your business objectives, it must gain support from the top. In order to achieve positive results, the CEO must be involved and active in the process. Succession planning is most successful if it has the full support and participation from the CEO. A highly engaged CEO will bring greater performance of employees and a more coherent succession planning program. The future of an organization is tied directly to the development of its talent, so the CEO needs to be invested in this process. Change is going to occur, so CEO involvement and support can help an organization to stay ahead of the curve and adjust by being proactive and making decisions for the good of the company and ultimately, the good of its employees. In order for succession planning to work, everything an organization needs to do needs to be done in the context of human capital management and developing talent.

The talent drain that exists today is forcing organizations to make succession planning a priority. In this chapter, we described the seven most critical components of an effective succession planning process. The best-practice organizations included in Part Two of this book have relied on the seven steps to create a robust program that is tied directly to the needs of the business. When surveyed, these organizations identified "driving organization alignment both domestically and internationally" and "building a development mindset" as the two most critical components to any succession planning system. When identifying their greatest challenge in succession planning, the majority of these organizations selected "ensuring data-driven decision making." Despite the challenges, these organizations have provided the tools, instruments, and methods that have enabled them to create a strong talent pool and a career path for their employees. They recognize the importance of viewing employees as assets. They have made succession planning a priority and instill the belief that identifying, developing, and retaining talent is essential to bringing companies great results.

Each case study includes the following features:

- A business strategy for the succession planning system
- A strong employee focus
- Program design and implementation to fit the needs of the organization
- Feedback and analysis
- Performance results

Part Two

BEST PRACTICES IN SUCCESSION PLANNING

3

BRIGHT HORIZONS FAMILY SOLUTIONS

Case Study

Bright Horizons, a company specializing in child care, early education, and work/life solutions, serves as a shining example of a firm that was forced to adapt and modify its succession management program in response to a rapidly changing environment. After having experienced a 100-percent increase in market size over a five-year time span, it became apparent that a formal bench system needed to be implemented. It is oftentimes the case that a large-scale change in company size represents a sizeable obstacle to even the most well adjusted of managers. Bright Horizon's receptiveness to this change and its ability to react quickly makes it a perfect scenario for rapidly advancing businesses that are unexpectedly growing out of their previous methods and practices.

This case study introduces the reader to the unanticipated occurrences that forced the executives at Bright Horizons to reevaluate their strategies. In addition to this, it provides an in-depth look into the variety of ways in which this company was able to assess the situation and produce adaptable solutions. Exhibit 3.1 provides a background to the chapter.

The Twelve Learning Elements

Bright Horizons handled two of the fears by developing the twelve elements and the 9 Block succession planning tool. The twelve elements represent the actions that exemplify the Four P's, establishing model behaviors to reduce ambiguity.

Exhibit 3.1 Bright Horizons Succession Planning Article

JANUARY 31, 2006

ON BRIGHT HORIZONS

"We don't make anything. We provide a tremendously important service through people. Great teachers make great centers; great centers are lead by great directors. People are our advantage," says Dave Lissy, CEO of Bright Horizons.

In the words of CFO Elizabeth Boland, Bright Horizons "is paid to make people's lives easier in a world that expects parents to be financially productive." The mission of this company is to provide innovative programs that help children, families, and employers work together to be their very best. They deliver programs and solutions in child care, early education, and work/life. Bright Horizons has partnered with leaders in financial services, pharmaceuticals, manufacturing, healthcare, technology, government, education, entertainment, nonprofit, and many other industries to form a community based on the caring and raising of healthy children into contributing and resourceful citizens. 88 Fortune 500 companies are Bright Horizons clients, as well as 54 of the 2004 *Working Mother* 100 Best Companies. Some Bright Horizons clients include Abbott Laboratories, Amgen, Boeing, Johnson & Johnson, Microsoft, Time Warner, and Wachovia.

BRIGHT HORIZONS AND INFORMAL SUCCESSION PLANNING

"In the past it was possible to be informal, watch the people who seemed impressive, get a gut read on potential leaders, observe who stuck out and promote from there. But we have doubled in size the last five years and are poised to double again. An informal approach isn't going to work anymore. We need to be systemic," states Dave Lissy. Growing from 8,000 to 16,000 employees in five years changes the dynamics and picture. And, more growth is on the horizon. It is expected that Bright Horizons will double their number of centers from 600 to 1,200 in the next five years. The scale is too big for adequate monitoring and attention via an informal process. Finding people with the requisite skills is getting more difficult. Having a predictable system is becoming more urgent. Mr. Lissy understands this need, stating, "This improved and systemic approach is logical to me and the executive team. We know that we need a solid succession planning process."

This logic became evident back in late 2004 when Bright Horizons held their annual senior management meeting, an opportunity to consult with the entire executive team. During the meeting the participants broke into small groups and reviewed the strategic challenges facing the company. It became clear during the small-group report-outs that developing people was

Exhibit 3.1 (Continued)

a key issue. Every single group reported it as essential to the growth and success of the company. It also became evident that a formal system, sufficient resources, and a common language were not in place. Clearly, this needed to be a top priority of the executive group. Dan Henry, the newly hired senior vice president of human resources (HR) stepped up to lead the effort with an eye toward building what would be considered a "world-class" approach to developing general management talent.

By the second quarter of 2005, Dan and his team had launched a global pilot of the Growth and Learning process for the top 250 people in the organization worldwide. The intent was to harness the energy and processes already in place and to redirect the efforts toward significant results. One of the first things Dan and his team did was to assess the current situation. Not long after the senior management meeting, they met with regional managers and division vice presidents to get their input and feedback about what was and was not working. They said that succession planning consisted of several fragmented efforts, specifically listing implementation in the field. The problem was that many directors and field managers brought their own forms and styles from previous companies and positions. At one point, managers identified at least seventeen different forms being used for employee appraisals. Consequently, that work didn't connect to any other system or process. Also, unlike other home office support areas, there was competency work in finance.

Competency maps were built for each position in the finance department. For each position, six to eight people were interviewed, competencies were developed, and the language wrestled with until all parties were satisfied. It was labor intensive. Furthermore, other groups asked that competency work be researched and completed, but with the company's fast growth it became too labor intensive to create and maintain a competency system. Also, the competencies were described in such a way that it was almost impossible for an employee to receive a positive evaluation even if the supervisor felt the employee deserved a positive review. The process displayed a great deal of shortcomings. "The previous system of competencies didn't work. It stifled conversation. It was almost impossible to receive good scores. The bell curve was too wide and there was no room for editorial comments," said Ms. Boland. Competencies were not the answer.

There existed a succession planning system in which all pieces and forms stood alone. Nothing was connected to a global architecture. At the top of the organization, succession planning consisted of the Leadership Development Program (LDP). In the LDP, people were identified by leaders to be a part of a working group that was to take on live business cases. As part of the LDP they had exposure to the CEO (Dave Lissy) and COO (Mary Ann Tocio) and had an opportunity to work on relevant business

(Continued)

Exhibit 3.1 (*Continued*)

problems. The LDP was intended to prepare people for leadership in corporate positions. Again, none of this connected. The LDP, competency work in finance, and appraisal process in the field were unrelated. The overall system was helpful but fragmented.

Finally, some employees had no development process or succession planning. Anybody who was in a function or field support role, or anyone in a center below the director position, fell outside the various programs. The next step was clear. It was necessary to get all the employees involved and to develop a connected, aligned, and scalable system. All the intent, systems, and processes needed to be harnessed and coordinated. The leaders of the company needed a way to align, measure, and promote the potential talent, development, and advancement of employees. Because language is so critical when leading large-scale change, one of the first tasks was to create a common metrics, language, and framework that was effective yet simple, professional yet intuitive. In addition, technology needed to be created to support, enhance, and distribute the new concepts and systems to a highly distributed global workforce. It was a big task and took eighteen months.

CREATING A CONNECTED, ALIGNED, AND SCALABLE SUCCESSION PLANNING SYSTEM

In the process of creating this language and framework, Bright Horizons developed some cornerstone concepts and language. The first was identifying several areas of focus and their importance to the organization. They identified four key areas. The first area is *people*. This area focuses on developing people and is referred to as "Heart Leadership." It is an organizational contract of behavior. The second area was *performance,* specifically financial performance and company growth. The third area, *partnerships,* stresses the need to interface and serve multiple groups or customers, including children, parents, partner companies, and internal entities. The fourth area, *programs,* emphasizes the tangible product of education and development for children, aids to parents, and related services. Consequently, there are Four P's: People, Performance, Partnerships, and Programs. The Four P's provide the backdrop and criteria for leadership within the company. The ultimate performance question is, "Can a person deliver against the Four P's?"

Herein lay the next challenge for Bright Horizons. Now that the Four P's were developed, how could they be given more breath and depth?

Dan spent time interviewing each of his colleagues on the executive team to get them to spell out in clear language "What would you see if it was happening or not happening?" This effort helped to define behaviors across twelve universal learning elements. Each element was subdivided into three

Exhibit 3.1 (*Continued*)

categories: learning, growing, and teaching, with specific language for each category. The team then created two simple versions: one for all field-based roles and one for all roles supporting the field.

Though there was no common language or process regarding succession planning, there were common fears. One fear concerned evaluating people in general. How does someone evaluate a person in a way that invites a conversation and growth instead of fear and defensiveness? Is it possible to separate the person from the results? Another fear was giving people feedback without being able to provide a way to help them develop. It is one thing to tell a person to improve but it is another thing to help them and/or provide the necessary resources. Resources to help a person perform were not readily available. Finally, people said the Four P's were helpful but did not provide enough specifics. This created a reluctance to use the system due to ambiguity. The Four P's needed more depth to become the framework for aligning actions and behaviors.

Dan envisioned one way to create more specifics. He understood the need to separate the *What* from the *How*. "If I hire a painter and he paints the house very well with no drips and excellent application he has great skills, but if he paints it the wrong color I get a bad result. That result is below target. It is possible for the painter to have great potential but provide below-target results. This is the separation of the *How* from the *What*, the potential from the result, the person from the behavior." With this understanding and distinction leaders and supervisors could begin to have candid conversations and feedback sessions that acknowledge a person's potential while providing honest observation and, if necessary, criticism.

They are spread across the Four P's and provide the necessary detail about expectations (see Table 3.1). Four elements comprise People (effective communication, managing performance, guiding the development of others, and leading by example); three elements make up Partnerships (effective and respectful partnerships, responsiveness, and change management and flexibility); three make up Performance (financial management and growth, effectively managing expenses and budgets, and leveraging financial information); and two elements complete Programs (quality of care and service, and world-class fundamentals).

Table 3.1 The Four P's and Their Elements

Four P's	Twelve Learning Elements
People (Heart Leadership)	• Communicating effectively • Living the "heart" principles • Supporting the growth and learning of others • Managing performance
Partnerships	• Forming strong partnerships • Providing exceptional customer service • Demonstrating flexibility and change management
Performance	• Understanding the Bright Horizons budget model process • Using financial information • Acting as a good steward of company finances
Programs	• Achieving excellence • Exhibiting job knowledge

Furthermore, each element is detailed by specific behaviors that are observable and actionable. As a result, they are general enough to be a part of all positions but written in a way that brings out the uniqueness of each employee role. As an example, the element of "Change management and flexibility" under Partnerships is tailored depending upon the position. In the home office for IT (information technology), this element states one thing, whereas for Center Based Leadership it says another. This also holds true for the other eleven elements. The wording of each element is geared to the position and/or role. With this as a guide, each supervisor can clearly determine the knowledge, skills, and attributes (KSAs) that an individual possesses and create a development plan for what needs to be accomplished. In this way, Bright Horizons has been able to build a system that is both universal and specific.

"The Four P's and elements are different than competencies in several ways. First, they are more general. The Four P's and elements represent a skills assessment with a broader brush. Competency work is more specific and position focused. Second, the elements are more flexible and less time consuming," says Dan. The organization's intent is clear with each of the elements, so there is alignment, but each supervisor, guided by that intent, can tailor the language to fit a specific position. And, each manager in the system maintains his or her specific language and form. The system does not require the labor-intensive development (interviews and writing) or maintenance. Third, the organization's strategy elegantly complements performance evaluation through the Four P's and elements. Exhibit 3.2

Exhibit 3.2 Performance Goal Setting Growth and Learning Plan

GOAL SETTING		
GOAL *What is expected?*	MEASUREMENT *How will you measure success?*	TIMING *Quarter/month*
PEOPLE (Heart Leadership) • Examples •		
PARTNERSHIPS **(Building "World Class")** • Examples •		
PERFORMANCE (Financial) • Examples •		
PROGRAMS • Examples •		

provides an example of their growth and learning plan. Every year the executive team develops the organization's strategy in each of the Four P's. Each manager can then translate the strategy into their own focus utilizing the Four P's and the elements as they relate to the manager's specific functions and tasks. In this way, Bright Horizons can leave the baggage of competencies, employing a system that is flexible and focuses on observed behaviors while being linked to the overall company strategy.

The 9 Block Succession Planning Tool

The other tool that has been developed is the 9 Block succession planning tool (presented in Figure 3.1). The 9 Block tool addresses many issues, including the fear of automatic defensiveness. The tool separates the *What* from the *How*, the person from the results, the potential from the performance. On the vertical axis is the person's potential. This describes the *Who*. Along the vertical axis is the *What*, the results. This axis describes the behavior and

Figure 3.1 9 Block Succession Planning

Potential for Success at the Next Level

High	Understand circumstances; address with job move, plan, support, and so on 7	Support in role and develop for next role 4	Short term 1
Moderate	Improvement plan 8	Support in role and challenge with new assignments 5	Long term 2
Low	Move out 9	Support in role– value 6	Special recognition 3
	BT	OT	AT

Performance in the Current Job

what has been observed. This tool allows for a conversation about observable behavior that distinguishes the person from the performance. It does not eliminate all defensiveness but it does address the performance issue as observed behavior instead of perceptions or subjective references. It eliminates the judgments of intent and focuses on results.

How does the 9 Block work? What would a 9 Block session look like? In a recent executive meeting the division vice presidents (DVPs) used the 9 Block to discuss and evaluate talent. This is how the session worked. The 9 Block was enlarged into wall-hanging posters 3 feet by 8 feet (the size of a normal door). Each DVP listed his or her direct reports on the chart in their respective positions. They placed their reports (employee's name on a Post-it note) in the presumed spot on the poster. The spot was determined by the intersection of the person's potential (vertical axis) and performance (horizontal axis). More specifically, the vertical axis measures a person's perceived potential in the next position or promotion. It does not measure their full human potential, only their potential for success in the next step up. The horizontal axis measures a person's observable performance and measured results. It is not uncommon for a DVP to gather the 9 Block data months in advance. Each DVP knows she or he will need to back up their reports placement with direct observations, specific examples, and measured performance results. This data needs to be directly relatable to the Four P metrics. "How is this person performing on the Four P's? How can I demonstrate that performance? How do I justify their potential for success if promoted or advanced?" These are the questions each DVP needs to answer with data.

The DVPs manage more than 15,000 employees. Their direct reports number 150+ potential leaders. The poster held more than 150 names and every name was discussed. This is the next level of power regarding the model. Every DVP justifies their "reports placement" in front of the entire executive team. Consequently, through candid and open dialogue two things happen. The placement of reports on the poster changes according to debate and consensus. Second, the open nature of the exchange slowly aligns the thinking, language, and assessment of talent. The dialogue creates calibration and understanding. By the end of the session, not only do people agree about who are the top leaders, ready for promotion, but they agree on what is important regarding leadership. Finally, the entire executive team knows the pipeline of talent available to the organization. The whole group can see the big picture from a people perspective. This leads to proper planning and adjustments as needed.

The succession planning process is short on forms and heavy on conversation. It also promotes accountability. When the process is repeated one year from now, the old poster is recreated. The entire leadership team looks at the old board, then builds the new board. The DVPs have a strong incentive to develop their people and to demonstrate that development through clear data. A conversation with their peers is coming, and such a group is a powerful force of accountability. Every DVP is motivated to show how his or her reports have developed and improved.

The Growth and Learning Program

The overall process is entitled the Growth and Learning Program (GLP). This is the umbrella that covers the overall succession planning program. The language is intentional. Each person is in one of three areas with each element: learning, growing, or teaching. A person in the learning stage needs to develop his or her skill and behavior in that element and seek out "learning" opportunities. When a person is in the learning stage, she or he has a development need and may look to people in the teaching stage of that element or go online to the Bright Horizons University for a course or developmental aid. People are in the learning stage when they never or infrequently perform the behaviors in an element. Thus, they need to "learn" those behaviors. Once a person is performing those element behaviors on a regular basis, he is in the growing stage. In the growing stage, the employees are frequently practicing the behavior and are well on their way to becoming role models. They have "learned" how to regularly perform those behaviors and are consistently demonstrating them. They are on the "growing" path, which takes them to the stage of teaching. In the teaching stage the person always performs the element. He or she consistently performs the proper behavior and creates the desired results. As a matter of fact, the person can be presented with a novel challenge and still create the desired results. She has not only "learned" and consistently performs the behavior but can create the necessary behaviors and results when put in a new and unforeseen situation. This is broken down in Table 3.2.

The Bright Horizons Growth and Learning Program (GLP) is a roadmap to support growth and learning throughout the organization. It is designed to help an employee in his current role while preparing him for any future roles. Each employee has

Table 3.2 Stages of Growth and Their Outcomes

Development Stage	Observable Outcomes of My Growth
Learning	I observe that this person almost never or very infrequently does the things listed under each learning element. He/she needs more time to grow and learn in the learning element area.
Growing	I observe that this person almost always or very frequently does the things listed under each learning element. He/she is well on the way to becoming a role model for the learning element behavior.
Teaching	I observe that this person always does the things listed under each learning element. He/she is a role model and would have credibility if asked to teach this behavior to others.

an individualized GLP that includes an assessment, a learning plan, annual goals with measurable performance indicators, development appraisals, and a career development pathway. This comprehensive process assesses, prescribes, reviews, and measures a person's progress relative to the Four P's and the twelve elements. It defines the way each role contributes to the success of the company and indicates what future roles will require. It both helps the employee in her present position and lets her know what will be needed as she advances through the company. Thus, each employee should know, at any given time, where they are. The 9 Block will show them whether they are below target (BT), on target (OT), or above target (AT). It will also show them their perceived potential for promotion and advancement. In one chart, two important items are measured regarding succession planning.

The five stages of the Growth and Learning Program are simple. The first stage is goal setting. Where does the employee want to be in six months' or one year's time? The next stage is job performance appraisal. Where is the employee right now? The skill and learning assessment, the third stage, informs an employee of his or her present status. Completing these first three stages leads directly into the Growth and Learning Program. This is where the online university, Bright Horizons University, or BHU, is such a valuable resource. The Growth and Learning Program, through BHU, allows the employee and supervisor to build a tailored series of courses and interventions to move the employee from the present to future state. By knowing the present state (where I am right now) and the future desire (where do I want to be in one year?) the employee and supervisor can practically plan how to move forward. The planning is the *how*. It is where the skill and learning assessment and Growth and Learning Program come into play. This stage happens at least once, if not multiple times, a year. It is a dynamic process that can be repeated at customized intervals. The fifth and final step is the succession planning stage, which

Exhibit 3.3 Performance Appraisal

Name: _____   Position: _____

Review Due Date: _____   Date of Review: _____

Supervisor Name: _____   Overall Rating: _____

Choose One: Supervisor/Self   Choose One: Six Month/Annual
                                                      Review

"As leaders in our field, we are committed to continuous growth and improvement." HEART Principles

Indicator	Performance
Above Target (AT)	Consistently outperformed the goals that were assigned for the year.
On Target (OT)	Met and often exceeded the goals that were assigned for the year.
Below Target (BT)	Met some but not all of the goals that were assigned for the year.

utilizes the 9 Block tool. In this stage the leaders in the organization assess the talent and development of the entire organiztion. Part of such an assessment includes performance appraisals. A sample appraisal is shown in Exhibit 3.3.

The Technology That Supports the System

One advancement for the entire Growth and Learning Program is the technology platform. Bright Horizons has developed an online solution that is now available to all employees; it is both comprehensive in scope and flexible (see Figure 3.2). In order for the company to have a dynamic process, technology was needed. Now an employee can update, review, and track progress throughout the year. The technology provides both a pull and a push strategy. The online system permits the supervisor to push assessment and goal setting and also allows the employee to pull for courses, tracking, updates, and additional feedback (see Figure 3.3). It encourages development to be an ongoing process

Figure 3.2 My GLP

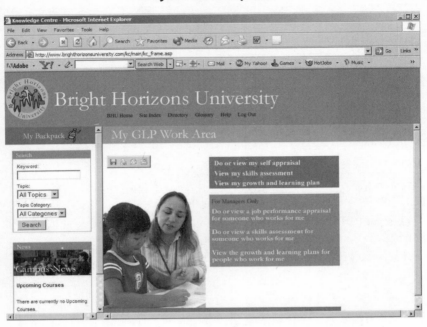

Figure 3.3 Job Description

instead of an annual event. The forms are simple yet effective. The online system is intuitive and practical.

Conclusion

The challenge Bright Horizons faces is creating a financially strong (publicly traded) company while providing a "high-touch" service of care, education, and child development. It is necessary to deliver this service in a cost-effective manner without sacrificing the quality of compassion and concern for children. How does Bright Horizons develop a caring, high-touch culture that permeates the organization while providing necessary and sometimes difficult feedback to employees and leaders? Can "high touch" and bottom line live well together? The answer is yes, and it is found in the practicality of the Four P's, the Growth and Learning Program, and how they are all linked from executive team strategy down to the individual development plans. It is practical and accessible. It is also scalable and flexible. It is the best of many programs. It is simple and effective.

Lessons Learned

This in-depth case study of Bright Horizons, focusing on the problems they faced as a growing organization and the solutions used to alleviate their growing list of concerns, is meant to serve as a reference for growing businesses faced with the same problem. Here are some of the main points of the chapter:

• A number of different issues could create a necessity for a formal succession planning system. It is important to note that Bright Horizons had a previous "informal" succession strategy that worked adequately for quite some time. The factor that caused this company to reassess their situation was the fact that they had experienced a 100 percent increase in scale over a short period of five years, essentially growing out of their previous practices.

• The previous succession program used by Bright Horizons was rather informal; it simply involved keeping an eye on key potential. To create a succession strategy that is self-sustainable it was necessary to develop a formal and specific plan that accounts for the identification, retention, promotion, development, and cooperation of vital company players.

• It is important to note that this company was successful in identifying the problem and creating a solution for one reason: communication. As stated at the beginning of the chapter, the problem came about in an annual meeting, involving all of their business executives, in which "participants broke into small groups and reviewed the strategic challenges facing the company." It is necessary, in this case, to realize the value of frequent business evaluation in identifying key problems.

• The Four P's, the first solution devised by Dan Henry, represents a big step in succession planning. The main significance of this strategy was the fact that it created a standardized list of company priorities to serve as criteria for employee evaluation. If all individuals are assessed based on the same list of elements, that eliminates the need to have a different program for each department.

• The twelve learning elements constituted a significant step in improving the previously established Four P's program. This addition to the Four P's was important because it eliminated any ambiguity associated with the system. It established a list of behavioral models that served as an indicator of outstanding performance. This allowed for key talent to be accurately and quickly identified based on positives rather than negatives.

• The 9 Block succession planning tool was also an essential part of the succession plan. This idea, used in a collaborative sense involving meetings of all division vice presidents, allowed for employees of all different departments to be compared on the same chart by the same standards of performance. This was also a big step for Bright Horizons because it was required that every employee ranking be addressed by consensus and discussed at length, making DVPs accountable for their own decisions.

- The Growth and Learning Program is a system that can easily be overlooked, but is absolutely crucial to creating a selfsustaining succession system. It is not simply enough to identify key talent and set up a bench system of replacements. One largely important aspect of succession, which is addressed by this system, is planning out and ensuring the development of the key talent identified. If potential champions are continually learning and developing, there will always be an ample supply of qualified potential.

- Bright Horizons University was an online application that allowed for consistent learning for key potential. Rather than simply relying on learning sessions, this application served as a constant and omnipresent educational tool rather than an incremental program. This allowed for a more gradual and more reliable rate of employee development.

- It is important to understand the significance behind these programs used by Bright Horizons. It is also important to look at the proposals in this case study in a critical sense. Ask yourself, What works with these systems and what doesn't? Would this succession program work in my company? Why or why not?

About the Contributor

Greg Zlevor is the founder of Westwood International, a company dedicated to executive education, consulting and coaching, and is the founder of the Leadership Project at Boston College for undergraduate students. He regularly works with both small and large Fortune 50 companies. Recent clients include Intel, Volvo, Honeywell, Johnson & Johnson, the Federal Government and GE. He has published several articles and is recently published in the *Change Champion's Field Guide.* He is a regular contributor to multiple leadership conferences including the Global Institute for Leadership Development.

4

CIGNA

Case Study

CIGNA, a health and employee benefits company out of Philadelphia, is implementing an entirely new and innovative succession process. This chapter provides an in-depth timeline of the events that led to the successful conception and organization of this new process, and provides an example of the specific foundations of a succession planning system.

CIGNA's story provides a step-by-step look at the amount of work necessary to create an interactive succession tool, and can therefore be a valuable resource for companies on the verge of a drastic step such as this.

Chapter Outline

CIGNA Introduction

A brief overview of the company itself and its status within their industry.

In the Beginning . . .

Brief historical overview of past succession process.

The Foundation of Change

Business situation leading to change in succession strategy.

The Start of Something New

Overview of the initial blueprints and business case leading to the conception of CIGNA's succession strategy.

2004 Succession Review: A Single But Bold First Step

Covers the one-day meeting that occurred in October 2004 that signified the beginning of CIGNA's road to success.

2005: Blueprint Enterprise Succession Process and Leadership Development Framework

Succession formats in detail.

The "52-Week Formula": Building Bench Strength for Increased ROI

Overview of CIGNA's model to promote depth within the organization.

Moving Forward . . . You Get What You Measure and What You Focus On

Focuses on the importance of employee development in creating a versatile and readily available bench system.

Lessons Learned

A brief recap of important points.

CIGNA Introduction

CIGNA, headquartered in Philadelphia, Pennsylvania, is a health and related benefits company with a comprehensive portfolio of health, pharmacy, behavioral, dental, disability, life, accident, and international businesses. With a net income of $1.44 billion for 2004, CIGNA has established itself as a business that is committed to protecting the health and well-being of its members and customers and is the provider of health and wellness benefits choices that employees need and expect. CIGNA also provides employers and consumers with access to technology, information, and services that enable education and choice. Through benefits programs and creative solutions, CIGNA enables employers to control benefits and costs and maintain a healthy, productive workforce. With more than 26,000 worldwide employees and 134 offices in ninety-eight U.S. cities and operations in fifteen countries, CIGNA provides coverage to millions of people globally and is a partner to 91 percent of Fortune 100 companies.

In the Beginning . . .

CIGNA has a history of conducting annual succession reviews. In years past, for each business segment the process entailed reviewing staff at least two management layers below the chief executive officer (CEO). The corporate requirements consisted of no less than nine templates and in most cases a lengthy written narrative overview as a cover note. Reviews were conducted at the CEO level through a one-on-one session with each direct report of the CEO and his or her human resources (HR) business head. The executive vice president (EVP) of HR and the head of leadership development were also present at each meeting. Considering that CIGNA was organized as a holding company that permitted business segments to operate fairly independently, the one-to-one business-by-business review approach did not seem out of kilter. But there were talent development barriers and real succession problems in this approach. Talent typically grew in silos, which turned out to be problematic for those in smaller business units. In these smaller units, people often felt gridlocked or shut out from being considered for roles in other businesses. Hiring managers were less eager to take development risks on people moving from one business segment to another. This was not ideal for retaining high performers. That's not to say that people never moved to cross-business roles; they did, but usually after protracted time and demonstrated expertise as "seasoned pros" in their role. It was a slow, development-risk-averse process. As this path was further used, the agility of the talent pool eroded, leading to significant limitations in bench strength. As a result of this it was oftentimes necessary to tap into the open market for talent, increasing expenses for the organization and posing a far greater risk to filling key positions. Employee development relied heavily on training programs and less upon testing people in new stretch developmental roles. But in late 2003, things started to change.

The Foundation of Change

CIGNA's business went into turnaround mode. Stock price was dropping, resulting in a loss of market share. In response, the organization structure was shifted away from the holding company model to a more nimble "One Company" operating mode. Rather than operate in business silos, the One Company strategy required more integration of people, processes, and systems. Over time the CEO's staff (executive management team, or EMT) started to be reformulated with several internal high potentials appointed in key roles. And, a new external EVP of HR was hired after twenty-five-plus years of the department operating under the same leadership. The business turnaround, several new EMT members, and a new HR head provided real momentum for making changes in the succession process and talent management strategy. The aggressive drive toward a One Company mindset (replacing running business segments that had been run in a silo mentality with more of an integrated company perspective) set a very important business context for how leadership development and the succession process would be revamped. Interestingly enough, during the height of the business turnaround, there was a sudden flow of talent from healthier business segments to the one in need. The urgent need for talent in one segment simply overshadowed the previous concerns of transferring someone more quickly than normal into a stretch role for which the person had limited specific experience. This flow of talent would become a useful lever as the new leadership development and succession model emerged.

As CIGNA was reinventing itself from an overall business strategy, organization structure, and executive leadership perspective, there was also a significant concurrent change going on in human resources. A new senior HR team was ultimately appointed along with a new head of leadership development and a new head of total rewards (compensation and benefits). Taking the lead from all the change in the business direction and operating model, new pay-for-performance compensation and career management systems were unveiled in 2004. The introduction of a new performance management model, new companywide career architecture, and introduction of career bands (the consolidation of dozens of job grades into seven broad categories, or career bands) would serve as an additional catalyst for how CIGNA grew its own internal talent pool to combat the war for talent.* These changes revealed a picture showing that CIGNA was undergoing sizable revamping, and human resources itself was at full throttle change.

The Start of Something New . . .

As the heads of HR and leadership development began to design the "blueprint" of a new succession review process for greater alignment to the One Company operating model, a few key objectives were pinpointed that were fundamental to the thinking process at CIGNA:

1. *Succession reviews are not about filling out data capture templates and having a "chat" with the CEO.* The former succession process was overly cumbersome and, by being a one-to-one CEO-business head conversation, did not reinforce the One Company strategy, nor was it as responsive to building a more agile talent pool.

2. *An effective succession review is not a "one and done" type of effort. (Conduct succession people review . . . and then stick the book on a shelf.)* Observations indicated that the succession plan was not viewed as a human capital operating plan due to the fact that people moves and development actions were not well correlated to what was discussed during the one-on-one succession review. As a result the succession plan was typically not used as the primary reference document for making talent deployment and development decisions.

3. *The most provocative succession reviews are the culmination of several ongoing parallel processes that include individual talent*

---

*The introduction of career bands provided an opportunity for employees to seek new development *experiences* (sometimes lateral moves) rather than just focusing on small incremental upward moves from one job grade to another. For CIGNA, the consolidation of dozens of job grades into more substantial roles enabled more access and fluid movement for employees seeking new stretch development roles, which served as a catalyst for increased employee engagement and a more robust talent pool. This is discussed again later in the chapter.

assessments, driving specific development action plans, performance management feedback, and consistent implementation of an organizational "theory of the case" for development. The succession review process is the culmination of the daily push for getting the right people in the right jobs, at the right time, and for the right development reasons. Succession bench strength and retention notably improved in pockets (within the organization) where this mantra was followed.

Tools that were built to actualize the third objective are presented later in the chapter.

As the business case for the new succession model was being built, the organizational context for change was derived from the following:

1. As CIGNA went from a holding company operating model, where businesses were run more independently, to a more highly integrated One Company model, the opportunity to parallel this change became an important lever for talent management across the organization.

2. The vitality of a more integrated organization depended even more on developing top talent via increased opportunities for cross-business/cross-functional experiences. The more CIGNA become an integrated team across the company the more premium they placed on people with enterprise and talent. It was very important to articulate this as the CIGNA leadership development operating model and to drive accountability for this with the executive leadership team.

3. The former succession process was cumbersome and often lacked common standards across the company. Corporate HR used to distribute general directions, but for the most part businesses tended to reinterpret the guidelines.

In addition to this, business heads were not required to have an enterprise perspective on succession backup talent nor an enterprise mindset on talent development. However, this all changed as a result of the One Company approach. Due to this new environment, succession review standardization across the enterprise (same formats and review process) would take on important new meaning and deliver more alignment to support an evolving new business culture.

2004 Succession Review: A Single But Bold First Step

In 2004, CIGNA was immersed in its business turnaround and was intent on instilling more of a One Company, synergistic culture across the enterprise. This started to really take hold in midyear. Significant work was underway across the company to find points of greater integration internally and externally. By the time the succession review date for 2004 was agreed upon, it was late summer. Fortunately, it provided the opportunity to let some of the new culture percolate before making the suggestion to alter recent succession review history at CIGNA. The major change for 2004 can be seen in Table 4.1.

During the full, one-day meeting in October 2004, each business head was required to share an overview of their organization's people strengths and weaknesses and provide action plans for shoring up talent gaps.

The CEO-EMT group discussion proved to be a powerful intervention. More conversation about providing development experiences across boundaries occurred, which led to several different optimization decisions. This was a significant signal to leadership that talent needed to be viewed as an enterprise resource and not the human capital of any one business leader. It also reinforced a very important leader development cultural artifact that had lost some momentum over the previous few years. The internal development model that had grown four out of six of the organization's' current business heads was centered on each of these individuals having their own unique set of cross-business and cross-functional (that is, sales, underwriting, finance) learning

Table 4.1 CIGNA's Major Change Made in 2004

From	To	Objective
1:1 succession review discussions with CEO and each business head, HR business head, executive HR head, and leadership development head	All CEO directs reports (EMT) together for a roundtable people review/succession discussion Included HR head and leadership development head	Strong reinforcement message of new "One Company" culture builds even greater business integration mindset • Drives more common understanding of key talent across enterprise • Enables more cross-business and/or cross-functional moves for talent development • Group discussions help to calibrate talent more fully than single point of view

experiences over time. By organizing a roundtable discussion it helped to revitalize and formalize the value of cross-developing people to grow a more ambidextrous, nimble talent pool.

Feedback from the EMT-CEO group session by attendees indicated that the roundtable format was the right model and was in sync with CIGNA's overall integrated strategy. Attendees appreciated the value of sharing information on their key talent and collaborating on optimum development strategies. Lessons learned from this session also shaped the bigger changes implemented for the 2005 succession process and for cascading the One Company succession process to lower levels in the organization.

It's also important to note here that the CEO agreed to a midyear (June 2005) succession/people follow-up review discussion. The purpose was to open another roundtable dialogue to discuss progress against commitments from the full review in October 2004 and to discuss other key people priorities pertinent to talent optimization and business strategy. Clearly, this established the direct link between what was discussed in the full succession meeting and implementation. This seemingly simple intervention is one of the ways in which the return on investment (ROI) of the process was driven. Immediately following the October 2004 review, follow-up action items were distributed to all executive staff attendees and the HR head, along with a note regarding a midyear follow-up. This was a significant step considering that CIGNA had a history of a one-on-one follow-up reporting process.

February 2005: "Blueprint" for Enterprise Succession Process and Leadership Development Framework

In February 2005, Leadership Development and the head of HR presented to the CEO a more complete enterprise-wide process for succession reviews that cascaded to the fourth employee layer (see Figure 4.1). This seamless process involved four data capture/ discussion formats (same four formats used in every business) and roundtable discussions at both the EMT and senior leadership team (SLT) management levels. The guidelines required each SLT member to conduct a roundtable discussion with all his or her direct reports. This session would then be followed by a roundtable discussion lead by each EMT member with all of his or her direct reports (SLT) looking at data collected from each SLT member's own previous roundtable discussion. Ultimately, data from each EMT-SLT meeting is forwarded to leadership development for

Figure 4.1 CIGNA's Succession Reviews Process

CEO	
EMT (Executive Management Team)	Layer 1
SLT (Senior Leadership Team)	Layer 2
Direct Reports to SLT (staff of staff)	Layer 3
Direct Reports	Layer 4

preparation for the final CEO-EMT review in October. Leadership development prepares a review book for each EMT member containing all of the executive management team member submissions. Review books are distributed days in advance of the meeting in order to allow for familiarity and discussion preparation.

Subsequent to the CEO meeting, leadership development met with each EMT member and his or her HR head to preview the new enterprise "blueprint" for succession and to renew commitment to CIGNA's overall leader development framework. As a summary, the succession process presented as Exhibit 4.1 was presented and agreed to, as changes for 2005 and beyond.

Exhibit 4.1 Succession Process 2005 and Beyond Overview

1. Roundtable discussions will become a standard protocol at the SLT layer (Layer 2). SLT members would require their direct reports (Layer 3) to complete succession data on their direct reports at the fourth layer. This would represent a change in many cases in which the SLT was meeting one on one with their staffs. The 2005 succession process would be the launch for a seamless enterprise succession review across all of CIGNA's businesses and down to the fourth layer of the organization. The same process and same formats across the company aligned to CIGNA's integrated operating model.

2. Introduced a leadership profile to accomplish several things:
   - Drive more focused, fact-based discussion regarding accomplishments
   - Inspire performance against CIGNA's shared values and desired leadership behaviors
   - Draw attention to the link between the annual performance rating and CIGNA's potential and performance 9 Box grid (shown in Figure 4.4), and
   - Provide more structure to development action planning by including a destination role

3. An *emerging leader* was defined as an individual with an annual performance rating of "E" (exceptional top performer) and who is placed in Box 1 (exceptional/high performer) on the 9 Box grid.

4. CEO-EMT meeting in October was expanded from one day to two days.

5. Annual succession review process calendar distributed in July to all EMT members and their HR head with guidelines on cascading the process to the third layer within each organization (direct reports of senior leadership team).

Succession Formats in Detail

Succession Chart: Format 1

CIGNA's succession chart (see Figure 4.2) requires nominations of backup candidates both in the "ready-now" and one- to two-year time frames. No non-CIGNA employees are permitted to be loaded as backups, as observations from the past use of external candidates indicated that these individuals may not be truly viable and could often be a "smokescreen" for not growing internal talent.

The Leadership Profile: Format 2

As referenced earlier, the leadership profile (see Figure 4.3) debuted in 2005 and became the discussion focal point during the succession review. An important factor regarding this format is that it not only

Figure 4.2 CIGNA's Succession Chart

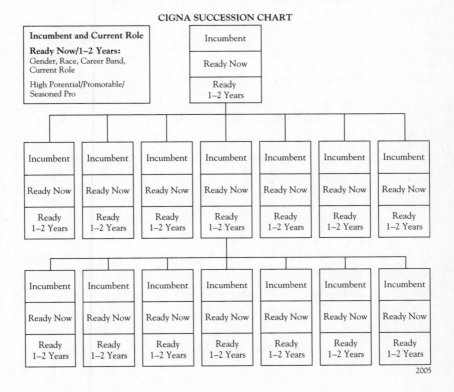

CIGNA SUCCESSION CHART

2005

Figure 4.3 CIGNA's Leadership Profile

Format 2   **CIGNA Leadership Profile**   CONFIDENTIAL

A. General Information

Name: _____

Business/Dept: _____

Time in position: _____

Current Role and Career Band: _____

• 9 Box: _____

• Current Performance
  Rating: _____

B. Shared Values/Leadership Behaviors   *Needs Improvement / Solid / Exceeds*   **C. Accomplishments**

	Needs Improvement	Solid	Exceeds
Value 1 Customer Driven	❑	❑	❑
Value 2 Urgency	❑	❑	❑
Value 3 Competitive Excellence	❑	❑	❑
Value 4 Respect	❑	❑	❑
Value 5 Integrity	❑	❑	❑
Value 6 Personal Accountability	❑	❑	❑
Ldr Beh Populate The Environment With Best People	❑	❑	❑
Ldr Beh Sets Clear Direction	❑	❑	❑
Ldr Beh Create An Environment That Challenges	❑	❑	❑
Ldr Beh Reward For Performance	❑	❑	❑

Accomplishments: ❑ ❑ ❑ ❑ ❑

D. Development Plan   Destination role: _____

Action plan for next 12–18 months: Be SPECIFIC in outlining development experiences required for further growth

---

became a guide for reviewing an employee, it also became a useful reference document to those who are unfamiliar with the individual. Additionally, by requiring some assessment of shared values and leadership behaviors, CIGNA was intentionally driving usage of a common language for how they "talk talent." (Each shared value and leadership behavior is operationally described and documented in the performance review system.)

9 Box: Format 3

The 9 Box format, a system of plotting employees based on their performance and potential, has allowed CIGNA to prioritize individuals on a uniform set of criteria (see Figure 4.4). Given a more comprehensive understanding of the positions that were in need of talent, it became possible to more efficiently track which employees to retain and where to look for additional backups. Using a box

Figure 4.4 CIGNA's 9 Box Format

Format 3

Performance

	Needs Improvement	Solid	Exceptional
High Potential	3	2	1
Promotable	6	5	4
Seasoned Pro	9	8	7

Potential *(vertical axis label)*

Too soon to rate/New to job

2005

format facilitated the process of implementing action plans. For example, succession reviews were limited to include only people in Boxes 1, 2, and 4, so that discussion could be focused on those employees in need of development strategies. With the discussion highly predicated on *action plans*, not just "show and tell," a stronger connection toward viewing the succession review as a people operating plan began to take hold. During each EMT organizational overview, there was also ample time to highlight other key individuals and people priorities.

An emphasis on action plans is important and should not be underestimated. A strong ROI objective of the succession review is not only the identification of backup talent but also to take action to assure continual readiness and/or to plan alternative development solutions when accession needs to be delayed. In cases where the incumbent is currently appropriate, alternative development action plans are required to keep the "ready-now" individual challenged. Danger lurks when a ready-now candidate is ready for a protracted period of time. If development action plans are not in place to keep this candidate highly challenged, vulnerability sets in and there is real risk of losing him or her to a competitor. Follow-up to the action plan is discussed at the six-month people review with CEO.

Emerging Leaders: Format 4

The objective here is to get an understanding of the very top "undiscovered" talent across CIGNA who have significant upside potential and who need to be placed on the organization-wide development fast track (see Figure 4.5). The theory is that if key potential is assessed properly, this cadre can be moved along more rapidly than other high performers. CIGNA deliberately set a high

Figure 4.5 CIGNA's Emerging Leaders Profile

Format 4

EMERGING LEADERS PROFILE

Name: Current role: Business: Time in Current Position: • • • + + + − −	Name: Current role: Business: Time in Current Position:
Name: Current role: Business: Time in Current Position:	Name: Current role: Business: Time in Current Position:

2005

performance and potential discrimination factor when identifying these exceptional individuals from those who are excellent high performers by requiring that they be a Box 1 (exceptional–high potential) and rated an "E" (exceptional) in their annual performance review.

At the CEO-EMT level, quite a few of these people were new news and were previously unknown, newly discovered talent. They are now on a leadership development "watch list" with the goal of accelerating their development and their exposure across the company. Leadership development staff will further calibrate these people to assess career runway and to serve as a catalyst, but the business heads and each HR business head take ownership for facilitating the development action plans for each emerging leader.

Within the Emerging Leaders Profile, the requirements are to specify the next two roles for further development along with timing and to briefly summarize key strengths and weaknesses.

CIGNA's Leader Development Framework

Included in the EMT-HR blueprint discussion regarding the roll-out of the new succession process, there also was an opportunity to discuss and reconfirm CIGNA's talent development "theory of the case." The overarching model for talent development at CIGNA is to continue placing a premium on employees who have cross-business/cross-functional experiences. One of the sure-fire ways to grow a career at CIGNA is to have had successful experiences in multiple businesses and/or functions. This message is directed toward all employees (included in CIGNA's career planning Web site) as they engage in career management and is discussed in CIGNA's Career Development Workshop. CIGNA has historically done this type of development, and it has paid off. The majority of their homegrown leaders have had experiences in cross-business and or cross-functional roles. During the EMT-Leadership Development blueprint conversations, everyone agreed to the concept of cross-business/cross-functional role switches as a framework for high potential development. As a result of this, necessity emerged for improvement in this area, providing a direct opportunity for leadership development to put several tools in motion to accelerate CIGNA's development strategy and work toward increasing succession bench strength.

The "52-Week Formula": Building Bench Strength for Increased Succession ROI

Earlier it was mentioned that a prime objective for the new succession model was to create a succession process that was not a "one and done" annual event. It was also noted that a succession review is really the culmination of yearlong *actions* that include identifying high potentials, implementing development action plans, and rewarding for performance by performance differentiation. Figure 4.6 displays some ways of building bench strength. To deliver on this objective, here is what was done.

Identify High Potentials

Leadership Development and CIGNA's EVP of HR agreed to orchestrate and sponsor a program to train HR generalists in a structured evaluation interview process through a program entitled "CIGNA Career Development Conversation Workshop." During this program, HR staff learned how to conduct a deep evaluation of an individual, produce a written evaluation, and recommend a development action plan that is shared with both employee and manager. The evaluation process is partially predicated on CIGNA's shared values and leadership behaviors (listed in Figure 4.3). CIGNA's leadership behaviors outline expectations on how leaders are expected to accomplish their objectives and set guidelines for how leadership is evaluated and defined. A key outcome from this program is the ability to deliver a *fact-based* assessment of someone's future career upside based on past performance as a predictor of future potential. The Career Development

Figure 4.6 Bench-Strength Builders

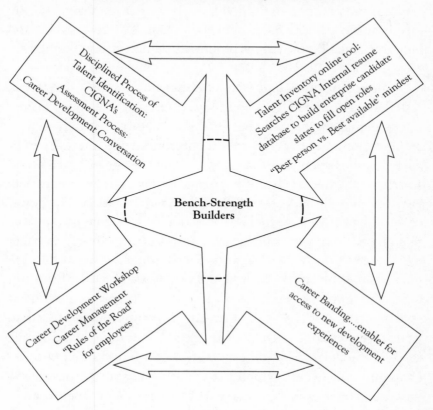

Workshop established a critical skill and technique for HR and has reinforced a common language (via CIGNA shared values and leadership attributes) for how talent is identified based on established criteria. The observations that have resulted show that HR staff and line managers are beginning to reconsider who they thought were their high potentials based on more structured in-depth interviews. Equally important is that people who were previously not well known began surfacing, enlarging the supply of people with career capacity. Another key outcome of this initiative is that once an individual is assessed as a high potential, the HR person conducting the assessment automatically takes partial ownership for partnering in the facilitation of the development action plan of this individual. The development action plan is a shared responsibility among the individual, his or her manager, and the HR professional. The focus here is on identification of talent and building an action plan. This process is a bench-strength builder.

Talent Inventory and CIGNA Internal Résumé. Designed, tested, and launched in 2006 was an internally developed online talent management tool that enables a database search against employee résumés to create robust enterprise-wide internal candidate slates for open positions. The "Talent Inventory" is based on searching an internal résumé populated with searchable career data based on pre-CIGNA and CIGNA career information. The power of the Talent Inventory tool is that no longer will open positions be filled based simply on who an HR professional or hiring manager can source through their network. Furthermore, a "network" candidate is possibly at the exclusion of others who have had the requisite experience based on work long since forgotten or while at another employer. The Talent Inventory permits queries based on years of experience correlated to CIGNA's function and family career nomenclature, other career areas of interest, other business areas of interest (both which help to drive a cross-business/cross-functional development framework) and several other career factors. The ability to inventory and then search on all the skills and experiences of an employee while at CIGNA and prior to joining CIGNA could provide a sizeable boost to the talent pool. The Talent Inventory does not replace CIGNA's active online job posting system. Instead, its search capability serves as a catalyst to identify and facilitate into new roles people who typically do not scan the posting system. In many cases, this is found to be true of upper-level employees who may need to be internally recruited and presented with new roles. The Talent Inventory is designed to be another bench-strength builder. In just one year, the Talent Inventory database had over 13,000 résumés, representing over half of the employee population. This inventory is proving itself to be a powerful tool for filling open positions and in identifying back-up talent for succession.

Career Bands. Launched in 2004, career bands at CIGNA moved the company from a cumbersome job grading system with hundreds of roles to a system of seven career bands with fewer, consolidated, and broader roles that are universally defined across the company. The move to career bands provided an "easy access" lever for employee development by eliminating the paradigm that new career experiences are predicated only on moving upward. With career bands, roles were expanded and progression from one role to another is encouraged based on the learning/experience value along with the business need. An employee is now more likely to take a new, possibly lateral role in a different function or business for development purposes without focusing on the optics of not moving "up an inch" to a new job grade with often marginal stretch. The emphasis is on learning and growing in bigger new roles creates further momentum to the theme of cross-business/cross-functional development.

Career Development Workshop. Launched in 2006 is the CIGNA Career Development Workshop. Within a few weeks, over 400 people had participated in a workshop. The objective of this three-hour workshop is to educate employees on universal career planning strategy, communicate CIGNA's development framework, and provide a thorough understanding of all of CIGNA's career management tools, such as the CIGNA career planning Web site and the advantages of career bands. In essence, the workshop represents a "bottoms-up" approach to informing employees about their personal accountability for managing their careers and imparting some universal career management practices. A desired outcome is to motivate employees to be on the lookout for new learning and growing development experiences. New workshop goals include making the content available on the desktop, and "lunch and learn" sessions.

The overarching objective of these "bench-building" efforts is to drive talent optimization by providing tools for HR staff and/or employees. The more awareness and know-how provided to employees to help them with career management, the more likely the possibility of stimulating and motivating employees in taking new stretch development experiences. The more successful learning experiences people add to their career portfolio, the more agile the talent pool becomes. This is not to advocate a constant ebb and flow of people in and out of new roles, since that is not an effective approach for business continuity. What is essential is that employees understand the development framework at CIGNA and, based on business need and their performance track record, are able to actualize their development objectives in a way that is a win-win. Likewise, providing tools for HR also provides momentum to driving action plans to maximize the identification, deployment, and development of CIGNA's highest potential.

Moving Forward: You Get What You Measure and What You Focus On

In preparation for the CEO-EMT succession roundtable in October, 2006, leadership development prepared several analyses as baseline data for setting objectives to measure annual progress.

• *Using Format 1: Succession Chart* (see Figure 4.2). A gap analysis was conducted to note the number of positions without ready-now or one- to two-year backups. This was used for discussion purposes and is used as a baseline measurement going forward to note progress on closing gaps.

• *Using Format 3: 9 Box* (see Figure 4.4). An assessment was made of who was listed in Boxes 1, 2, and 4, with highlights on diversity and notable trends. An ideal 9 Box would be populated with a majority of backup talent sitting in Boxes 1, 2, and 4.

Additionally, the expectation is that each senior HR staff head will do this same analysis (using Formats 1 and 3) for their own respective organizations to establish a baseline for measuring improvement. Leadership development collaborates with each HR business head, and their direct reports help improve baseline metrics by facilitating the identification and development of top talent.

Overall this data will be used as part of a scorecard to measure enterprise progress on building a succession bench. The war for talent requires a laser focus on identification and development, and is bolstered by a strong sense of determination along with key metrics to chart progress. With new tools in place to educate and engage employees in how to grow their career portfolio at CIGNA (Career Development Workshop), and with several important new HR tools to identify and assess talent (Career Development Conversation Workshop) and to help drive employee development across the enterprise (CIGNA Internal Résumé and Talent Inventory), it is believed that this provides a distinct advantage on the "talent battlefield."

As employees come to understand how to grow their careers at CIGNA, the expectation is that employee engagement will rise, allowing for the growth of a more versatile talent pool to help build succession bench strength.

CIGNA has been and continues to be passionate about growing its own cadre of leaders through strategic deployment of its best and brightest into new stretch development experiences. The executive management team is heavily weighted with talent grown from within, and the objective going forward is to recapitulate that pattern across a sizable number of leadership roles at various levels. The enterprise process and requisite tools have been established, and with visible leadership commitment to achieve this objective CIGNA believes it is well on its way to achieving success.

Lessons Learned

This case study on CIGNA exemplifies the specifics of planning and implementing a succession plan. Although there is no particular conflict in this study, it accurately depicts the amount of work and collaboration necessary for such a bold move. The main points of the chapter are summarized as follows:

- CIGNA did have a succession plan previous to the one described in this case study. It was inadequate, however, for several reasons. The biggest problem with the old system, apart from the fact that it only involved two layers of employee monitoring, was that each department was in charge of applying its own methods. This led to an inefficient process of succession management and also served to perpetuate any silo conditions that were prevalent throughout the organization.

• The main driver for the implementation of CIGNA's new system was the adoption of their "One Company" approach. This differs from the previous case study in that, rather than conflict, this organizational change was a result of a drastic change in company culture. This One Company mantra, stressing the importance of merging the departments into a cohesive group, created a necessity for a succession procedure that involved uniform practices throughout the entire firm.

• One of the reasons for the success of the CIGNA program is the fact that they pushed several universal strategies on their executives. The first was that they understood the inefficiencies of one-to-one meetings in dealing with succession. Rather than stick with individual CEO-executive meetings, they pushed for a new collaborative group approach. This forced each member of each department to adopt a universal system of criteria and language while also holding every member of the group accountable for their own decisions. The second point is that these succession decisions were originally made on an incremental basis, or using a "one and done" approach. For a sustainable program in succession it is oftentimes important to utilize a system that allows for continual (rather than periodic) evaluation and modification as well as fluid decision making.

• The CEO was critical in driving the succession process. It is often the case that the CEO is an essential and integral part of an initiative such as the one outlined in the chapter.

• Another important point is the in-depth look at CIGNA's talent development program. This should be considered in great detail as talent development is a strong basis for a successful succession initiative.

- The 9-Box Format used by this company is very similar to the 9-Block format used by Bright Horizons described in Chapter Three. This is an interesting similarity. CIGNA made use of it by first prioritizing the boxes and then organizing individuals into the boxes. Once this was accomplished it showed which employees were in need of development action and which were worthy of retention.

- As stated in the previous chapter, one should read with a critical eye. Were the actions taken by CIGNA the best solution for its scenario? Could this have been accomplished in an easier or more efficient manner, involving fewer people in the decision-making process? What would you do in this case?

About the Contributor

Harriet Phillips has twenty-four-plus years of human resources experience with a concentration in leadership development and staffing. Harriet has spent the majority of her career at General Electric (GE Aerospace) in a variety of senior HR leadership roles and ultimately held division headquarters responsibility for succession planning and talent development for the thirteen businesses within GE Aerospace. Following GE, Harriet joined the corporate staff of Citigroup, where she was responsible for building the global leadership pipeline for human resources. Presently Harriet is the head of leadership development for CIGNA Corporation in Philadelphia.

Harriet presently serves on the Undergraduate Advisory Board of Cornell University's Business School. She has undergraduate and graduate degrees from Temple University.

5

ALLIEDSIGNAL

Case Study

Succession management can be the most powerful tool for transforming a business—when a company creates a systemic focus on building talent throughout the organization and on a global scale. Honeywell International, formerly known as AlliedSignal, saw the value of this tool and used it to create a complete organizational turnaround.

In 1999, a merger combined two businesses into one international organization. The two companies, AlliedSignal and Honeywell, formed a Fortune 50 conglomerate that became known as Honeywell International. As a result of this merger, it became apparent that the company had embarked upon a business venture that stretched its resources among a wide variety of different industries and products. The chief executive officer (CEO) at the time, Larry Bossidy, had the foresight to know that a broad organization such as Honeywell International would be spread too thin to be managed by one leader alone. Thus, succession and development of a deep talent bench came into play.

This chapter can serve as a valuable guide to overcoming the challenges of managing a rapidly expanding business entity.

Chapter Outline

A Business Imperative

Outlines the business case, or company need, for the creation of a new succession program. Makes an account of the first step of AlliedSignal's transformation, the gradual creation of an entirely new corporate culture with an emphasis on "people focus."

Forming Priority Principles

Shows the elements that must be in place for the succession plan to succeed, the principles set up by the company to form a foundation for the changes to come. Also looks at the hard work and the essential commitment for AlliedSignal to do the right thing and eliminate company complacency.

Providing a Forum for the Task

Outlines the mechanisms and tools created to facilitate executives and managers in adopting corporate priority as their own. Also shows the role of HR in implementing the company succession strategy.

Getting Things Down in Black and White

Looks at the MRR, a mandatory forum that served as an organizer and agenda for executives to use in initiating their strategies. Includes information about AlliedSignal's intense discussion and evaluation process and the role of the CEO within it.

Success via Succession

Reviews the results and rewards from AlliedSignal's effort and sacrifice.

Lessons Learned

Recaps of the more important aspects of the case study.

As they seek to transform a company, CEOs typically turn to a toolbox that contains a limited number of instruments. These often include cutting costs, buying and selling operations (usually in an effort to gain some sort of quick fix), pumping up marketing expenditures, or expanding sales efforts. Choosing yet another, longer-term approach, CEOs can also decide to key a turnaround with new products and new technology, and flood research-and-development with new dollars and new energy.

During the mid-1990s, AlliedSignal, which became Honeywell International, counted on quite a different lever to accomplish a deep, lasting overhaul of the company. *Succession planning* and a focus on human capital management became the key driver behind AlliedSignal's overall transformation strategy because the leadership team embraced the view that the company being built would only achieve long-term success if the right calls were made about people and their development. Further, they had to emphasize the importance of this discipline throughout the company. Nothing was more important to developing a competitive advantage than executing these principles regarding the acquisition, development, and deployment of talent.

AlliedSignal always enjoyed a good supply of capable, even brilliant, people. But the company's performance was lackluster, as measured both by business returns and by a lingering stock price. It lacked a clear, strategic roadmap for success. A large conglomerate operating in many industries, with units of a broad range of sizes and with locations around the world, AlliedSignal was simply too complex to be led by only one fantastic executive at the very top. Success for such a far-flung organization required highly capable, decisive, ambitious managers in many different places. Furthermore, they all had to be organized in an appropriate manner and advance toward strategic objectives. Honeywell lacked that.

When Larry Bossidy took over as CEO, people and commitment to execution became the focus of his transformation strategy. And while Honeywell certainly recruited a good number of individuals who could help right away, it was realized that the greater payoff would come from establishing a vibrant internal development and succession planning process and mechanisms within the company. One problem was that Honeywell indeed already had many great managers on board, but a huge share of them were buried in the organization and were either not being developed or not being listened to. It was determined that the best way to help Honeywell become more successful was to help make internal talent more successful.

Under Bossidy, this emphasis on developing people had become part of AlliedSignal's bedrock corporate culture by the end of the decade. However, it was severely tested in 1999 when AlliedSignal merged with Honeywell, creating a newly merged entity called Honeywell International—a Fortune 50 company with $25 billion in sales and technical and product leadership across a wide range of industries including aerospace, industrial controls, transportation products, and materials. Nowadays, Honeywell provides aerospace products and services; control technologies for buildings, homes, and industry; turbochargers; automotive products; specialty chemicals; fibers; and electronic and advanced materials. The corporate goal was to create one strong company, with extensive operations worldwide, from a collection of disparate industrial concerns.

The results spoke for themselves. The transformation of AlliedSignal was recognized at the time as—and has remained—a remarkable success story in the annals of corporate America. Just as significant, there's a cavalcade of ex-Honeywell top executives who now are leading other companies and who honed their approach to talent development and succession planning in large part at Honeywell, including CEO Fred Poses of American Standard and former CEO Daniel Burnham of Raytheon. In addition to this, companies led by executives who were steeped in the culture of development and succession at Honeywell are among the best prepared in America for an era in which talent increasingly is the most valued currency of the business realm.

A Business Imperative

Through the 1980s, AlliedSignal was a typical industrial conglomerate, continually lagging in terms of performance, whose executives mainly peered into that conventional toolbox for things that would elevate the company to the next level. The company's focus was on buying and selling businesses and operating in the right markets, so AlliedSignal was continually involved in mergers and acquisitions. But some executives were undermanaging their businesses, and as a result progress became stagnant and the company began falling behind its competitors.

A major but unacknowledged weakness of the company was that there was a lack of a systemic "people focus" in the organization, as is the case in so many struggling companies. This problem was recognized in part because there wasn't a robust or consistent performance appraisal process at AlliedSignal, and there was little transferring of talent among the company's various businesses. Human resources (HR) existed in a functional silo that was built around traditional HR concerns such as labor relations and benefits management. And while there certainly were some great managers and promising people throughout the organization, there was no development mindset about unleashing the talent that lay within the ranks of the company.

This all changed when Larry Bossidy arrived as CEO in 1991 from a leadership role at GE, and AlliedSignal began its fateful shift. During the first eighteen months of his tenure as CEO of AlliedSignal, Bossidy traveled throughout the company, communicating and listening, and sharing his vision of the importance of good people and flawless execution. He spoke to 15,000 people the first year, presenting his vision, explaining markets and strategies, engaging in debate—in short, teaching. It was just the beginning of a process that transformed not only people management within AlliedSignal but also the company's entire culture and its strategic orientation. Bossidy began instituting an orderly process to harness, grow, develop, and fully leverage the talent within the organization.

Beginning with Don Redlinger, corporate vice president of human resources, the company began to operate under the philosophy that high-performing companies get that way by betting on people first, then on strategies. The emphasis was that a thorough, meticulous, and action-oriented succession planning process was the most important way to ensure that AlliedSignal had the right people in the right places to achieve the short-, medium-, and long-term results that were desired. Their experience underscored an important reality for HR professionals: The only way to earn a seat at the corporate table is by teaching and helping drive the importance of succession management throughout a company and by highlighting how it achieves business results. This is certainly easier with an enlightened line executive, it can be easier to do—but in that case, expectations of HR's performance in this regard are even higher.

A dramatic example of how this focus on people development worked can be seen in the story of Fred Poses, an employee of AlliedSignal for about twenty years, whose unique gifts blossomed after Bossidy arrived at that company. Poses already had a deep knowledge and passion for AlliedSignal's business, as well as great commercial instincts. He also placed a strong focus on detail and execution, but held HR in rather low esteem. In running the company's multibillion-dollar materials business, Poses realized he needed better people to improve the operation. So Poses took a page from Bossidy's book and decided to hire a strong HR executive, and Bossidy began mentoring Poses in the importance of a people focus. Soon, Poses was championing and benefiting from the positive effects of people upgrades all around him. After flourishing in the company's new people-centric culture for several years, Poses left in 2000 to head American Standard, which he has led to new heights.

So, as executives thought about and acted on what businesses to starve or feed, the company's thinking started with the people inside each organization. They focused on inventorying their ranks, systematically making people better, forcing their leaders to be accountable for their progress, and deploying them in optimal ways. There was also great importance placed on linking employees and succession strategies with business strategies, specifically through the notion of continuous improvement.

Despite its strengths as a company, AlliedSignal was in dire need of operational improvement. Standards weren't high and the company wasn't operating efficiently; for example, AlliedSignal didn't have modern supply chain management. Purchasing often was done entirely on a price basis, not because the procurement decision fit some larger vision for the company's progress. Strategies for growth weren't clear, based often on hope versus sound thinking.

With the mindset of overcoming those operational weaknesses, they began to raise the bar steadily on their expectations of both operations and people, with the idea of leveraging the movement of people into and out of various jobs as a catalyst that would advance each business operation toward its performance goals as it enhanced the career of each executive and manager.

In other words, talent management became the new means of achieving results, thinking strategically around a portfolio of talent and where it was placed.

Particularly illustrative of this approach was the automotive business. Today, auto suppliers are under even more pressure in a mature and intensely competitive business, but things were pretty stark even in the mid-'90s. U.S. automakers that were Honeywell's primary customers had been losing big chunks of market share to Asian and European rivals; the original equipment manufacturers (OEMs) had begun drumming suppliers for significant annual price concessions even as the company was supposed to take over more of the product development work from their customers, causing costs to rise.

Instead of just asking the question, "What do we do to fix it?" with an action plan oriented around assets and operations, Honeywell answered with a remedial strategy that in large part revolved around human resources. They resolved to restore the business by moving in people who could handle the challenge and moving out those who were part of the problem—as well as by developing a plan to feed the right people into the business in the future. Instead of taking the conventional approach of turning elsewhere in the auto industry for help, players from high-performing companies where the culture emphasized succession planning, such as GE, Emerson, and PepsiCo, were brought in. The company brought in people who seemed to possess the will, skill, intelligence, drive for results, and cultural fit to take its auto business to the next level—even if they didn't have experience in that business. Talent deployment and succession planning were used to change the nature of the game.

In addition to this, AlliedSignal enshrined training and skill development and overall learning as an important value within the company. For example, every employee of AlliedSignal was expected to participate in at least forty hours of some sort of learning, from traditional classroom instruction to internal "internships" in the field. New learning centers were constructed on the headquarters campus of AlliedSignal in Morris Township, New Jersey, as well as in Europe and Asia. The investment in bricks and mortar was an important signal to everyone in the company about the long-term importance of learning. AlliedSignal raised the competence level of all who attended these centers; Bossidy himself spent roughly 20 percent of his executive time teaching his charges, and he expected all of his direct reports likewise to spend 10 percent to 20 percent of their time teaching.

Because of what was accomplished in this area, AlliedSignal/Honeywell generally became known as an "academy" company. Perceptually, this put them in the same ranks with General Electric, PepsiCo, Proctor & Gamble, and just a few other U.S. corporations that had become breeding grounds for talent development, not only benefiting the companies themselves but also raising the overall quality of leadership of corporate America.

As this new strategy grew, even relationships with customers directly benefited from AlliedSignal/Honeywell's palpable intensification of their interest in talent development and succession planning. Not only were better people sent out for them to deal with, resulting in more understanding and responsive service, but also they perceived this rising competence as a reliable indicator of a supplier that was advancing in a general sense as well. Some of them even started benchmarking Honeywell's talent development process by sending people to examine their practices.

Forming Priority Principles

It was one thing to declare that talent management and succession planning would be primary vehicles for moving both AlliedSignal and Honeywell forward, but the most important aspect of the flourishing of this culture was the cold, hard fact that executives and managers were required to treat people development with far more than mere lip service. Its importance was woven into every aspect of leadership and management of the company, through seven primary principles.

Universal recognition that this would be the operating philosophy was the first important element of making it work. Everyone from Bossidy on down made it clear that a strong commitment to talent development and succession was at the very core of the culture, and that everyone was expected to contribute their utmost to the effort. Everyone was responsible for building their own benches—not just business general managers but those in finance, sales, marketing, and HR as well. Every executive and manager recognized—and top leadership continually acknowledged—that this would be far from the path of least resistance; that there was substantial risk involved in using succession as a primary transformative lever. To make this work, much sacrifice would be required. It was clearly established that discipline and hard work were going to be required for AlliedSignal to realize extraordinary success with this unconventional approach, and the board and management team never wavered from their conviction that it was the right way to go.

If executives didn't accomplish certain specific actions to which they had agreed as part of development and succession planning, it became a major red mark against that person, with potential implications not only for his or her bonus but also for future compensation and advancement. If a leader was handicapped in that particular aptitude, she was expected to make sure that her human resources manager could support her and help her with her shortcomings. Yet executives weren't allowed to shift accountability for executing this priority to HR: Everyone was responsible for building his own bench and for contributing to the company's overall bench strength.

The second element was the *determination to provide executives and managers with honest feedback*. The company implemented a robust performance appraisal process that ensured every manager worldwide would receive specific performance objectives, every year, and it was emphasized that this appraisal would always be the most important way to assess their performance. At the end of each year, each manager was measured against those objectives and given specific feedback. Additionally, for the head of each of AlliedSignal's more than twenty business units, there was a requirement to spend as much time as necessary reviewing people development and succession plans and to require his or her charges to do the same, right down to the bottom of the organizational chart. They were then held fully accountable for implementing them.

The evaluation process was nonbureaucratic and comprised a very direct aspect of the relationship between bosses and their charges. Yet the company's approach was entirely fact based. Objectives for each manager or executive were clearly iterated and the metrics agreed upon; their performance against these goals served as the continuing basis of discussion throughout the year. If an executive professed that one of his or her charges was destined for better things in the company, that leader was expected to figure out what this promising individual required to get better and realize his potential, and then express it in specific recommendations. If the first actionable recommendation, for example, involved a transfer of the executive overseas, his boss was expected to begin to talk with the executive about the type and timing of such a move and to ask about and help address the potential issues affecting the family. Then, it was up to those in HR to work with that executive and ensure that the transfer actually took place.

Besides suggesting who would move where, and when, and outlining specific moves and action plans, these evaluations also would serve as the launching pad for other positive results. For one thing, with a thorough understanding of each division's portfolio of talent, the executive in charge and her lieutenants could always discuss in full knowledge and confidence how they could use personnel moves to meet business needs internally and how the talent they were developing might be able to feed other parts of the company. Also, employees themselves could count on getting thoughtful and well-considered input about their strengths and weaknesses, and they would receive responsible and clear direction about their future with the company, delivered honestly and forthrightly with plenty of room for their own feedback and an opportunity to discuss conclusions.

A third critical factor in enshrining this philosophy was that *the defined scope for AlliedSignal's talent development process was worldwide*. Many U.S.-based companies mistakenly focus only on developing American talent, believing that they could be deployed to whatever operation abroad and best manage the indigenous managers. But AlliedSignal's goal was often to obtain the most talented native executive. And when a severe talent squeeze developed in the United States during the 1990s, AlliedSignal combated it in part by leveraging people fully on a global basis. At the same time, this worldwide sweep included necessary talent and customs respect for local market differences.

A fourth key enabler in ensuring buy-in from throughout the company was that they deliberately engineered and fastidiously maintained *a balance between the importance of human performance in the here and now and the future*, reassuring executives that meeting their operational goals was crucial and reminding them of the importance of talent development for the future prosperity of the organization. There was intense discussion and focus on having the right people in the right jobs today so that things could get done, as well as equal importance given to what executives were doing to develop individual careerists for tomorrow.

A fifth and very important principle, as people were used to transform AlliedSignal, was to make sure that *the best people were retained and developed, while those who were least capable of helping the company were culled out*. A threshold was quickly established in hiring "A" players; and careerists just as quickly came to recognize the fact that, if they came to AlliedSignal, it was like punching a future ticket to anywhere. "A" players like to work with other "A" players, and people were attracted to AlliedSignal for that reason. They also knew that they would be developed and presented with growth opportunities, not be lost in the shuffle. Not only high fliers, but steady, solid performers were highly valued, and made up the bulk of AlliedSignal's management and executive ranks.

A crucial aspect of building this corporate advantage was the notion of "tough love." Poor performers were treated with encouragement and support, but also with realism and firmness. They were confronted directly about their needs and their issues, and great effort was given to their development. The company's leaders also were savvy enough to realize that their organizational charts required the stability of having players in key positions whose greatest advantage might be their longevity, experience, and stability in those jobs, especially as the movement of other people was accelerated above, below, and around them. Ultimately, AlliedSignal's goal was to treat everyone in the organization with respect and dignity at all times.

One must be mindful, however, that one of the biggest mistakes companies can make in their efforts to demonstrate compassion is to demote people to their lowest levels of capability on a systemic basis. This tendency severely hinders succession management because it clogs up development opportunities in the organization for people with potential who must have these experiences in order to grow. For this reason and others, one of the worst things that an organization can do is treat their best- and lowest-performing people the same. So at AlliedSignal, rewards were differentiated among "A," "B," and "C" employees. The company made it clear to their steady performers, who constitute the heart of the organization, that they valued their contributions and wanted them to be able to improve. Meanwhile, the poorest performers received coaching. But there was no hesitation in talking with them about the possibility of their moving on and encouraging them to understand that they probably could be more successful with another company. If their performance didn't significantly improve, they would be asked to leave.

A sixth priority principle for AlliedSignal was to *stretch their high-potential executives and managers as much as possible*, a crucial dynamic in effective succession planning. One way of doing this was through training programs and other learning expectations. In their performance appraisals, each individual confronted one or two developmental needs that were considered important for their further career progress. At the same time, each operation within AlliedSignal had organization-wide developmental requirements that were tied to the strategy for that particular business. Managers and executives were expected to work proactively to ensure learning experiences against both types of goals for everyone under their purview.

A second lever that tended to tease potential out of careerists was to put these people on projects and teams that forced them to leave and perform outside of their comfort zones. But by far the most effective way of elevating the performance of a capable executive or manager to the next level was to put them in "stretch" assignments: new jobs that they *almost* weren't capable of handling at that point. Putting them in positions where the risk of failure was palpable, where its possibility was about equal to their chances of success, tended to light a fire within high-potential people and bring out their best. If an individual didn't quite perform in such a situation, the fact that the new demands on them had been so high made it easier to move them to a less demanding job for a time and allow them to regroup for their next charge up the organizational chart. Overall, their usual success in such situations became a powerful engine for operational improvement, competitive differentiation, and corporate transformation for AlliedSignal.

Finally, it was important at AlliedSignal that *the compensation for an executive or manager must reflect not only his or her performance against operating goals for the previous year but also his or her long-term value or potential to the company* as an individual. For example, an executive may have had a bad year, and it would affect his bonus for the year. However, this candid feedback was always delivered in the larger context of that individual's long-term value to the company. For example, in certain cases there was recognition that the executive had been put into a stretch job, and the expectation that he would perform better in the future would be accounted for. Developments outside of his control, such as an important customer not making its own numbers, were always taken into account. Yet, if that individual clearly was learning, getting better, and deserving the faith that was put in her, the company would load her up at the same time with equity in the form of long-term stock options. So while her compensation would take a short-term hit, that executive also would get the message that she was important to the company, and it would be backed up tangibly with rewards to entice her long-term devotion to AlliedSignal.

Providing a Forum for the Task

Having established talent management and succession planning as a corporate priority, and manifesting it in certain principles and expectations of management, AlliedSignal also had to devise, develop, and deploy particular mechanisms and key tools that would encourage and facilitate their executives and managers in adopting the priority as their own.

Most important in accomplishing this was the establishment of a human resources planning process as one of three equally important planning exercises for everyone in management as the year progressed. Managers were expected to present an annual operating plan, a strategic plan, and a human resources plan each year. Of those three processes, the human resources plan was the only one to which each executive and his superiors, along with an executive or manager from HR, devoted two separate sessions. Every fall, there was a session to assess how the individual was performing in his responsibilities for succession and talent development. Six months later would be a follow-up session that amounted to an evaluation of how well the executive had followed up on the action plans agreed to at the first human resources plan meeting. All of this was consistent with the principle of "execution" that Bossidy would come to have associated with his management style.

For HR professionals, their preparation for and execution of these sessions were especially critical. The discussions were the most important means of determining how well they understood the business and whether their action plans around people development were aligned with their business unit strategies. What was considered to be most important was the quality of the thinking that went into their presentations, not how cleanly they had completed the accompanying forms.

Overall, these sessions, known as Management Resources Reviews (MRRs), became part of the fabric of how AlliedSignal was led and managed during the '90s, and they comprised the core of a process that many other organizations since have benchmarked or adopted. Understanding their specific importance and the overall importance that the culture placed on development and succession management, these meetings and their results put energy and motivation into the company, a sense of purpose, and an intensity that encouraged engagement and drove performance. For example, if an executive oversaw ten different businesses, and there was great attention placed on the people management details of each one, the sessions became monumental events. Sometimes, these meetings would take eight or nine hours, but such marathons were, among other things, high testament to their importance.

Neither were the human resource planning sessions long just for the sake of length. Led by Bossidy and Honeywell's HR leadership, senior management forced their charges to prepare seriously and think through their answers thoroughly for very in-depth, action-oriented conversations about their people. Yet there was no real way for executives to rehearse for these meetings, because the discussion was too intense to allow them to set up such barriers. Obfuscation and side-stepping were not tolerated. Everyone was expected to offer open feedback. And in the end, senior leadership found out what was needed.

Those in HR had very important and very specific roles to play in advancing and supporting the company's talent management emphasis and these succession management reviews. At the very top levels of the company, for example, after each review with the president of a business unit, Bossidy, with the help of HR, would compose a synopsis of the key follow-up points. These were concise and agreed prescriptions with little wiggle room, and they were to be completed before the next human resources planning session six months later. Most important: six months later, the executive had to answer for the prescriptions that had been laid out in the two-page letter, to Bossidy himself, who unfailingly made the letter the focal point of that semiannual discussion. And if that individual hadn't been diligently implementing his or her talent management and succession agenda during that time, the implications were as bad for him as if he'd missed an operational or financial number.

Moreover, the integral role of HR in the strategic planning process also elevated their role in the transformation and direction of AlliedSignal/Honeywell overall, helping them to act and be perceived as a high-value partner of top management, not simply as a low-value, transactional-oriented support function. Those in HR were expected to formulate and put forth strong points of view about talent management and succession. Thus, if a business unit manager was savvy, he or she could adopt and be adopted by his or her HR executive as an ally, typically running the business day to day and executing the operational strategy while the head of HR was shepherding the unit's very important emphasis on developing their talent, exchanging it with other parts of the organization, ensuring robust procedures for filling the talent pipeline, and conducting and expanding training and executive education programs.

Getting Things Down in Black and White

Like many great systems of thought, AlliedSignal's approach also was embodied in a particular document, which was called the Management Resources Review. This was a form of several pages that

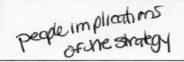
people implications of the strategy

served as an organizer for each executive's talent development strategy and execution and as an agenda for the human resources planning sessions. Taking this template seriously, and completing it individually, was the personal responsibility of every leader in the company—not just that of senior management or of the human resources department.

On page 1 of the MRR was a document that dealt with the people implications of an operation's business strategy (example presented as Exhibit 5.1). On the left side of the page the executive preparing the MRR would list the business issues, and on the right side of the page he or she would match each business issue with the human resources implications. If, for example, the unit was contemplating expanded marketing activity in China, listed as a business issue, then the companion implications for people might be "Hire 25 sales representatives in China" and "Fund Chinese marketing expansion by decreasing sales head counts in Western Europe." The point of this process was to give talent and succession issues an operational and strategic heft that had to be addressed.

Exhibit 5.1 People Implications of Business Strategy

Key Business Drivers 2006	HR Implications 2006
• Increase sales in Europe by 12% • Develop new NA markets for product X • Introduce PRODCO in Asia in 4Q06 • Streamline supply chain for 20% cycle time reduction	• Add experienced sales manager to regional • Complete product training for European sales team • Recruit sales leader with experience in consumer sector to lead market expansion • Upgrade capability of current Asia personnel to support launch • Conduct technical sales training for key personnel • Reassign 2 scientists for 12 mos. to assist with market development • Reorganize HQ logistics center • Shift technical team expertise from Cinc. to L.A.

Page 2 of the MRR was simply a collection of key macrocosmic statistics about the company and its people that described the health of the organization in human resources terms. This proved to be quite helpful in understanding the implications of talent development and succession decisions. These numbers would include counts of people in the United States and overseas operations, how many employees were new, a snapshot of the company's demographic diversity, and a "time and title" look at how long the organization typically was keeping individuals in their current jobs at various levels. The page would be combed for data that could inform further discussions of succession, and the information inevitably fostered questions once trained executive eyes could focus on it. They could determine whether the snapshot presented a picture of an organization that was structured consistently with their business needs and make decisions based on their conclusions.

Page 3 was a traditional organizational chart of the operation, with details such as when an executive started with the company and his or her current position. (See sample presented in Exhibit 5.2.) Taken together, they would form the basis for robust discussion of why an executive's business unit had taken on the form that it did, and whether that person was making the right personnel decisions and resource allocations in light of that. The organizational chart also would serve as the basis of discussion regarding the performance of the executive in terms of having a blend and a balance of people: those with valuable experience compared with those who still had the callow optimism of youth, those with street smarts and those with new ideas, those with right-brain orientations and those with left-brain. The organizational chart was studied intently to ensure that the structure logically followed and supported the executive's business strategy—whether it indeed depicted a deployment of his talent that matched how he was trying to take the unit forward. If the shape of the organization no longer made sense in light of that, the chart would be changed along with the structure of the operation. Another, supplemental chart within the MRR laid out "organizational design alternatives" (see Exhibit 5.3) that the business unit leader was

Exhibit 5.2 Organization Chart

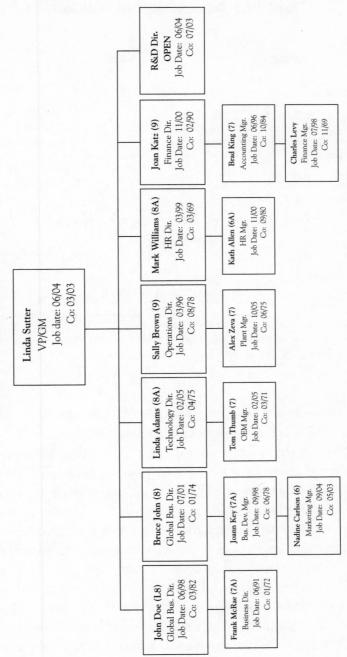

Linda Sutter
VP/GM
Job date: 06/04
Co: 03/03

John Doe (L8)
Global Bus. Dir.
Job Date: 06/98
Co: 03/82

Frank McRae (7A)
Business Dir.
Job Date: 06/91
Co: 01/72

Bruce John (8)
Global Bus. Dir.
Job Date: 07/01
Co: 01/74

Joann Key (7A)
Bus. Dev. Mgr.
Job Date: 09/98
Co: 06/78

Nadine Carlson (6)
Marketing Mgr.
Job Date: 09/04
Co: 05/03

Linda Adams (8A)
Technology Dir.
Job Date: 02/05
Co: 04/75

Tom Thumb (7)
OEM Mgr.
Job Date: 02/05
Co: 03/71

Sally Brown (9)
Operations Dir.
Job Date: 03/96
Co: 08/78

Alex Zeva (7)
Plant Mgr.
Job Date: 10/05
Co: 06/75

Mark Williams (8A)
HR Dir.
Job Date: 03/99
Co: 03/69

Kath Allen (6A)
HR Mgr.
Job Date: 11/00
Co: 09/80

Joan Katz (9)
Finance Dir.
Job Date: 11/00
Co: 02/90

Brad King (7)
Accounting Mgr.
Job Date: 06/96
Co: 10/84

Charles Levy
Finance Mgr.
Job Date: 07/98
Co: 11/69

R&D Dir.
OPEN
Job Date: 06/04
Co: 07/03

Exhibit 5.3 Organizational Design Alternatives

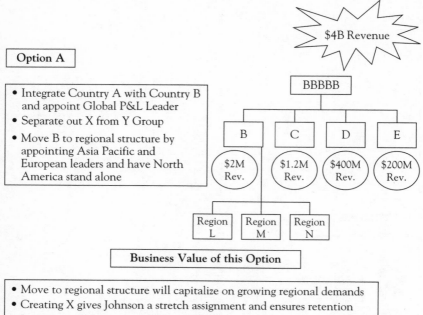

considering as ways to address aspects of the picture described by the organizational chart by reallocating resources.

Next in the MRR were the evaluations of specific individuals within the operation, the top ten or twenty people for whom that manager was responsible. These Continuous Improvement Summary Profiles (see Exhibit 5.4) captured on one page the most recent performance assessment results versus the attributes that had been deemed important, a summary of strengths and weaknesses, development plans, and career planning.

One of the reasons that human resources planning sessions could take so long was that this phase of the discussion was very important. When AlliedSignal's HR personnel sat down with Bossidy and talked with his leaders, a philosophical discussion wasn't what ensued. A specific action plan was formulated, including a precise plan for

Exhibit 5.4 Continuous Improvement Summary

Employee Name: Joe Smith   SUCCESS, ATTRIBUTES AND
                        VP Marketing   BEHAVIORS

SKILLS	EXCELLENT	AT STANDARD	BELOW STANDARD
Business Acumen	X		
Customer Focus	X		
Strategic Insight		X	
Vision and Purpose	X		
Values and Ethics		X	
Action	X		
Commitment	X		
Teamwork		X	
Innovation	X		
Staffing			X
Developing People		X	
Performance	X		

Results Overview

2005 Performance Highlights

- Relaunched brand X in Europe while growing volume 50%
- Opened new wholesaler avenues through innovative sales/marketing linkage

2005 Targets Missed

- Lost global accounts in Italy
- Failed to hire a Japanese marketing leader to support customer growth

2005 Challenges

- Execute against relaunch strategy

Summary Strengths

- Excellent business acumen and insight
- Sets high standards and acts as role behavioral model

Development Needs

- Needs to focus on coaching junior staff
- Move faster to upgrade poor performers

Development Plan

- Work with HR in the area of people skills – assign coach

Potential Next Moves (Short Term 0–2 Yrs.)

- Remain in current job

Potential Next Moves (Long Term 2+ Yrs.)

- With continued growth he can transition to line management and run a business people development toward outcomes that were also detailed. By the end of the session, the executive being evaluated had committed to well-defined actions and a precise game plan was taking flight.

Executives were also encouraged, in their evaluations of their own charges, to make not only general judgments about an individual but also very specific ones. From the top executive the company expected crispness in his or her assessments, and that they not only be backward looking, but also that they took serious stock of the evaluee's future. From such written evaluations, candid, penetrating discussions would flow. The bottom of the form was then checked to make sure the employee had signed it, because an individual's acknowledgment of his strengths and weaknesses, and of where that put him in the organization at that moment, was crucial.

The MRR also included two important grids that helped synthesize the rest of the data in the document and usually provided the most important snapshot of the state of talent development and succession planning within a particular operation. The Leadership Assessment Summary (see Exhibit 5.5) was a twelve-month assessment each fall of how each individual within the executive's

Exhibit 5.5 Leadership Assessment Summary

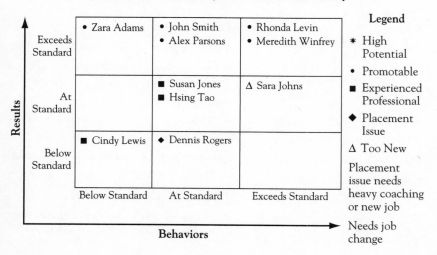

purview was performing, and in what manner he or she was getting things done. The y-axis of the grid was labeled "Results" or "Performance," and the x-axis was labeled "Behaviors." The Leadership Assessment Summary grid created four quadrants, and the executive placed each of his charges in one of those quadrants. Those who were considered both to have great results and to have achieved them in a way that encouraged their employees, rather than frustrated them, were placed in the golden upper-right-hand quadrant. Those who exceeded standards in performance but needed improvement in behavior, or vice versa, were placed in either the upper-left or lower-right quadrants. And the individuals who excelled in neither way and ended up "below standard" in both areas were placed in the lower-left quadrant, and were targeted for immediate and particular help to see if they could improve. This summary served as a key tool for evaluating the people management skills of the executive in charge of this operation and, in turn, for her in assessing the individuals in her operation.

The overall conviction was that the first job of a manager or executive was to hire and develop people who could some day take the manager's place, that the long-term growth of Honeywell was dependent on having lots of people who were ready to step up to the next level of responsibility and helping train them to succeed. At the same time, the company respected the roles, status, and value of seasoned professionals who weren't inclined to jump around and who added some necessary balance throughout the organization. Not only were they made aware of their value, but their development was continued and they were granted stock options, just as was done with those who were moving quickly around the organizational chart.

The next crucial page in the MRR was a list that depicted succession depth within the operation (see Exhibit 5.6), providing with undeniable clarity an answer to the question of how well an executive was developing his bench strength. Along the left side of the page, the executive would list all the positions for which he was responsible. The next column would list the incumbents in those

Exhibit 5.6 Succession Depth Document

Position	Incumbent(s)	Job Date	Succession Candidates		
			Ready Now	Ready 1–2 Years	Ready 2–5 Years
VP/GM	Susan Smith	6/04	Amanda Smith Alexander Green	Greg Jones	Eva Adams
Global Business Director	John Jones Sam Nadarajah	7/03 5/01	* Judy Tang	Steve Hem Jordan Allen	* Ali Ahmad
Finance Director	Tom Po	8/01	Mitch White Cassandra Bull		Michael Joseph
Technology Director	David Jason	2/99		* Sam Wall	Max Smith
Operations Director	Sara D'Amato	4/04	Jack Jill	Rhonda Jackson	
Marketing Manager	Jack Roberts	5/02		* Felix Rodriguez	
HR Director	Roberto Ferrari	4/98	Karen Lemon	Anne Perez	Elton Weaver

* Diversity incumbents and candidates

positions. The third column listed the starting dates in the job of each incumbent. The following three columns got to the point of the exercise: they listed specific succession candidates for each position, the first column being those who were "Ready Now," the second being those would be "Ready in 1–2 Years," the third being candidates who would be "Ready in 2–5 Years." If all of those "ready" spots weren't filled, or weren't occupied in ways that the executive could defend, it comprised a major priority for that executive to improve the situation.

The succession depth document told an important and concise story about the status of that executive's organization and could lead to some incisive conversation. If there was a hole in the chart behind someone who was considered to be a good manager of his operations, for example, a couple of possibilities could account for it. Maybe the executive wasn't a good people manager and had trouble keeping his management bench full—a definite red flag. Another possibility is that the executive was such a good developer of management talent that other units of AlliedSignal/Honeywell were constantly appropriating talent from her organization. Thus, the snapshot conveyed by this chart often led to very fruitful discussions about the status of the operation and the overall strengths and weaknesses of its manager.

Each MRR also included a number of other important documents that guided and facilitated discussion. One chart listed key vacancies within the business unit, each position matched with an "action plan" for addressing the gap. Another was a summary of the status of expatriates (see Exhibit 5.7), emphasizing their uniqueness and importance to the company. A summary of top talent within the unit was an important way to keep track of individuals deeper in the organization whom the leader believed were most worthy of promotion and to ensure against talent hoarding within departments. All of these documents intimately involved HR executives and depended on their having broad and deep knowledge of the company, and discussions around these forms always depended heavily on the views and insights of the HR team.

Exhibit 5.7 Expatriate Positions Summary

Name/Title/ Location/ Home Country	Job Grade	Assignment Reason				Start Date	Expected End Date	Potential Return Assignments	Previous Expatriate Assignment
		Project Work	Develop Leadership	Transfer Critical Skills	Fill Position				
Reva Shansky Marketing Mgr. (U.S.) Chicago Home: Poland	10		✓			1/05	8/07	Mktg. VP East Europe	None
John Doe Finance Director Shanghai Home: L.A., USA	8			✓		4/04	4/07	SBU CFO	Japan 6/95–6/98
Hsing Tung Plant Mgr. Beijing Home: Chicago	6	✓		✓		9/03	9/05	Ops Director China Ops Dev/ SE Asia	Hong Kong 6/01–6/03

One more chart specifically addressed the diversity of leadership and of top talent within the business unit, underscoring the corporate priority of growing a diverse organization (see Exhibit 5.8). Leaders identified a cadre of diverse candidates, both to inventory their talent within the company and to ensure that these individuals got enough training, exposure, and access to jobs. This chart provided not only a way to catalog and track those people but also to ensure that every significant discussion of a manager's performance would include an assessment of how well he or she was managing diversity.

A final chart summarized the business unit's priorities for the coming year and what role that personnel actions would play in achieving them.

Success via Succession

The precision of thought and execution that was encouraged by AlliedSignal's reliance on these tools, in turn, encouraged intense discussions and bold decision making based on their convictions about people management and succession. And, in turn, these attitudes and actions fueled the steady but very measurable transformation of AlliedSignal/Honeywell that had been the goal from the beginning. Between 1991 and 2000, shareholders recognized the company's stellar performance by pushing its share price to multiples better than the Dow Jones Industrial Average performance for the period.

Perhaps even more telling was the diaspora of executive leaders who were among the greatest "products" of the company's approach to succession management. They emerged from their tenure and training at AlliedSignal/Honeywell to take CEO and other C-level positions at other major companies, further utilizing and spreading the people-centric gospel that they had learned during their time with the company.

So, both the results at AlliedSignal/Honeywell and the success of executives they had trained were, in large part, manifestations of how they made a priority of talent management and succession

Exhibit 5.8 Diversity Talent Development

Top Talent: *Diversity Candidates Pipeline*

Name/Title/Job Date	Job Level	Time w/Co.	EEO	Retention Risk*	Next Job/Timing	Development/Retention Plan
Alan Adams Finance Mgr. 01/05	6	2/02	AA	Moderate	Finance Dir. In larger more complex bus. 6/07	• People development • Non-U.S. operations • Coaching/mentoring by David Hahn
Anita Rodrigues Sales Mgr. 06/04	4	08/94	H	Moderate	Latin America Sales VP 06/07	• Finance course for non-finance managers • Assign to re-launch project • Stock option grant
Hsing Chu Bus. Dev. Mgr. 03/01	5	07/86	A	Low	Bus. Dev. Director Asia Pacific Region 07/05	• Exposure to c. crew • Place in 12 mo. U.S. project assignment • Language coach

planning. The imperatives at work on and within American corporations today—including shorter tenures for leadership, relentless pressures from globalization, and the growing talent squeeze as baby boomers retire—suggest that more CEOs should take up Honeywell's example.

Lessons Learned

• In business it is normal for a company to experience a natural cycle of ups and downs. This case study describes a number of ways in which CEOs try to jump-start their ailing businesses through conventional short-term methods. One example of this is the fact that AlliedSignal frequently engaged in mergers and business acquisitions in order to create a positive shift in productivity. Imperatives such as these are not always successful; even when they are they generally do not make an impact that extends beyond the short term. After the merger between Honeywell and AlliedSignal, the company applied succession as a long-term impetus for corporate change. The success of this strategy serves as a testament to the necessity of long-term and out-of-the-box thinking when facing economic opportunity.

• It is important to note that this company did not solve their problems simply by creating and executing a succession plan. A large Fortune 50 firm, Honeywell International was forced to undergo a radical change in corporate culture. It was through the establishment of an entirely new business ideal that they were able to achieve the results they needed.

• To radically change the culture of an entire company, Honeywell was forced to follow a ground-up approach and extend a hand to each individual. To do this they implemented an objective requiring each and every employee to participate in at least forty hours of hands-on learning.

• One aspect of this case study that stands out is the essential role of the CEO in instigating this corporate change. It must be considered that it was the actions of the CEO, Larry Bossidy, that created the momentum necessary to create success within Honeywell International.

- This case study illustrates a slightly different approach from that used in previous chapters. It is mentioned throughout the chapter that rather than use a businesswide, collaborative approach, Honeywell International instead chose to hold all managers and executives individually responsible for those under them. These leaders each had to follow a singular method of developing their own talent, and in addition to that were subject to careful monitoring at all times to make sure that their potential was being properly developed. Leaders could leverage resources, policies, and programs in the larger organization for support. Make sure to make note of the requirements for each executive and manager in adhering to Honeywell's succession program and the methods that were used for keeping surveillance on individual talent.

- The most important factor of this company's succession strategy is the Management Resources Review. This review, consisting of both a meeting session and a physical report, was the most integral method of holding executives accountable for their own employees and ensuring management compliance with the overall business strategy. The meeting served a necessary role by forcing one-on-one discussion regarding the regular practices of the executive under review. As a result of this meeting, individuals had to formulate articulate responses about their methods with absolutely no previous preparation. The document portion expanded on this by adding documentation and record keeping to the entire succession process within each department. It also allowed for the formulation of goals and strategies.

About the Contributor

Dennis Zeleny has spent his career developing and leading human-capital programs that focus on improving individual and organizational performance for Fortune 50 global corporations, working closely with CEOs and top-leadership teams. He has directed human-resources transformation in a wide range of areas, including large-scale organization and culture change; mergers; acquisition integration; compensation and benefit design; corporate governance; talent acquisition, assessment and upgrading; executive coaching; organizational learning; team development; communications management; and building international processes for sustainable business enhancement.

Dennis began his career at PepsiCo and spent 17 years there in multiple assignments. He has headed human resources for some of the world's largest companies, including Honeywell and DuPont, and most recently has served as Executive Vice President of Administration & Services for Caremark Rx.

Dennis is an acknowledged expert and a frequent speaker about issues and trends in global human resources. He received a B.S. from Cornell University and an M.B.S. from Columbia University's Graduate School of Business.

6

LOCKHEED MARTIN

Case Study

Lockheed Martin is a company that has responded admirably to the so-called war for talent that began in the late 1990s. Headed by Lockheed Martin's former chief executive officer (CEO), and in conjunction with the company's human resource (HR) department, this organization was able to create a simple and effective long-term solution to build its leadership pipeline and lessen its need for external talent. The culmination of the efforts taken by these individuals is the Executive Assessment and Development (EAD) program, a well-planned program designed to manage and facilitate the proper development of high-potential directors and vice presidents within the organization.

This chapter takes an in-depth look into each aspect of the EAD program. Although it is significantly shorter than the other case studies, the Lockheed Martin example shows an incredible amount of detail relating to the development of talent and the evaluation of both applicable individuals and company initiatives. Therefore, it is highly recommended reading for anyone with an interest in either of those areas.

Chapter Outline

Background and History

Provides a brief look at the company in general, what caused its need for an efficient succession program, and who contributed to the development of this strategy. Discusses the overall goals of the resulting employee development plan, known as the Executive Assessment and Development program.

Target Audience and Participant Selection

Looks at the specific criteria under which leaders are evaluated for potential.

Program Components

Lists the different aspects of the EAD program and how they contribute to the development of key talent.

Measuring Progress

Shows the overall methods for evaluating both participants in the program and the program itself.

Summary

Briefly describes the tangible results of the program, which are few due to its recent implementation, and the lessons that Lockheed Martin learned as a result.

Lessons Learned

Recaps the important points of the chapter.

Background and History

With the "War for Talent" heating up in the late 1990s, Lockheed Martin's senior leadership acknowledged the need for a more proactive approach in identifying, assessing, and developing talent at the director and vice president levels. In 2000, former Lockheed Martin's CEO, made a commitment to enhancing the leadership bench strength of the corporation. He did this by working with human resources to create an accelerated development program for high-potential leaders called the Executive Assessment and Development program. The goal of the program is to identify high-potential directors and vice presidents who have the potential to be promoted one to two levels above their current positions or take on broader roles within the corporation. The program provides insight into strengths and development needs for the high-potential leaders. It achieves this goal through assessments, coaching, mentoring, developmental workshops, and action learning (see Figure 6.1).

While the EAD program is just one program that makes up an integrated talent management approach for the corporation, it marked the start of building enterprise-wide talent pools for the corporation.

In addition, prior to the start of the EAD program, there was no consistent and open acknowledgment of who was a high potential. The executive-potential candidates didn't know they were considered high potential and of course, did not know who else fell in that category from other parts of the corporation. After an initial pilot of approximately 20 vice presidents, in 2001 the program was launched with 120 vice presidents and directors from around the corporation.

Figure 6.1 Integrated Talent Pyramid

Integrated Talent Development Approach

Target Audience

Developmental Components

New President or Functional VP, EVP Potential → **Top Talent** ← Yearly focus on key people, Executive Coaching & Mentoring Focused Development Plans

VPs, Directors with BU President, BU Functional VP, or Large PM (VP level) potential → **EAD Executive Assessment & Development** ← Executive assessment & Coaching, mentoring, 360 assessment, Focused Development Plans, 2 week-Corporate Development Program, Action Learning

Managers with Director and Director-level PM Potential → **LEAD Leadership & Executive Assessment & Development** ← Executive assessment & coaching, mentoring, 360 Assessment, Focused Development Plans, 1-week Corporate Development Program

Business Unit High Potential Leadership Programs

Early Career Leadership Development Program

Target Audience and Participant Selection

Candidates nominated for entrance into the EAD program were high-potential vice presidents and directors who were thought to have the ability to work in positions one to two levels above their position and could manage roles with greater complexity, size, and scope.

As a part of the succession planning process in each of the businesses, executive leadership identified candidates who had the potential to demonstrate the following key management and leadership behaviors used as entrance criteria for the program:

- *Develops strategy.* This leader is able to develop a long-range course of action or set of goals to align with the organization's future direction.
- *Demonstrates entrepreneurial thinking.* This leader identifies and exploits opportunities for new products, services, and markets.
- *Thinks globally.* This leader integrates information from all sources to develop a well-informed, diverse perspective that can be used to optimize organizational performance.
- *Drives change.* This leader creates an environment that embraces change, makes change happen—even if the change is radical—and helps others to accept new ideas.
- *Advocates and develops talent.* This leader attracts, develops, and retains talent to ensure that people with the right skills and motivations to meet business needs are in the right place at the right time.
- *Motivates and inspires others.* This leader builds passion and commitment toward a common goal.
- *Mobilizes resources.* This leader proactively builds and aligns stakeholders, capabilities, and resources for getting things done quickly and achieving complex objectives.
- *Navigates through complexity.* This leader clearly and quickly works through the complexity of key issues, problems, and opportunities to affect actions (for example, leverage opportunities and resolve issues).

- *Supports the enterprise.* This leader ensures shareholder value through courageous decision making that supports enterprise- or unitwide interests.
- *Has the ability to manage profit and loss.* This leader demonstrates financial acumen, business knowledge, and technical knowledge.
- *Has a positive customer contact/interface.*
- *Has the ability to be engaged in a leadership capacity in the community.*

Program Components

The EAD program is two years in duration to allow an adequate amount of time to complete the assessment phase of the program, implement actions from development plans, work closely with coaches and mentors, and complete the program curriculum.

The program consists of the following components:

1. *Executive assessment.* The executive assessment consists of an evaluation of personality factors, interpersonal skills, management skills, and problem-solving abilities. This assessment, conducted by an external organization, was accompanied by a 360-degree interview-based assessment conducted internally by an HR professional. Verbal and written feedback were presented to the participant approximately four to six weeks following the assessments.

2. *Executive coaching.* An internal HR professional who had completed a coach certification partnered with the participant to assist in the preparation of a development plan that the participant was encouraged to share with his or her manager. When a final development plan was put in place, the coach began working with the participant as his or her coach over the course of the two-year program duration.

3. *Mentoring.* Participants in the EAD program were also assigned an executive mentor. The role of the mentor is to

offer advice and guidance to the participant in areas related to career, professional development, and job-related challenges or opportunities. It was important to distinguish the difference between the role of the coach and the role of the mentor so that expectations of each were clear (see Figure 6.2).

The participant's manager, coach, and mentor acted as a "development team" for the high-potential leader, as shown in Figure 6.3.

4. *Leadership courses.* All participants in the program attend two courses to enhance their skills in preparation for operating at a higher level. Each weeklong program was designed after a gap analysis was completed by reviewing group assessment data.

Figure 6.2   Role of the Mentor

Role of the Mentor	vs.	Role of the Coach
• Provides career development advice • Can provide broader understanding of the organization and/or profession • Shares experience, vision, insight in navigating the culture • May act as a sounding board for the development plan • May facilitate networking opportunities		• Engages in a relationship with the EAD participant that helps facilitate participant's development process • Synthesizes feedback for the participant and creates a clear and focused picture of the strengths, development needs, and possible courses of action for the individual • Acts as a resource for the participant by researching information and resources that will help them with their development needs by challenging their thinking in order to continuously enhance themselves as a leader • Leverages the wisdom and strengths of the participant in addressing development goals

Figure 6.3 Development Team

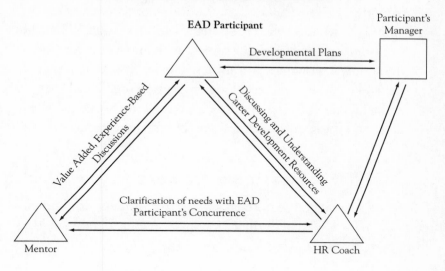

EAD Participant

Participant's Manager

Developmental Plans

Value Added, Experience-Based Discussions

Discussing and Understanding Career Development Resources

Clarification of needs with EAD Participant's Concurrence

Mentor

HR Coach

These courses give the participant insight into the ways of thinking and operating styles it takes to be successful at those levels while providing the individual an opportunity to network with leaders from other parts of the corporation. It also provides an opportunity to assess their interaction with others during the week. The content of each week is as follows:

- EAD I: *Strategic Leader Experience*. This is a five-day, highly interactive program that consists of information about current issues facing executives in the global, political, and legislative environment. Building on that, participants apply nine roles of a senior strategic leader in the Strategic Leader Experience—a business simulation activity conducted by Development Dimensions International (DDI).
- EAD II: *Executive Influence and Impact*. This workshop is the culminating event of the EAD program. It consists of information to help participants leverage their basis of power and influence, enhance their executive presence, and work on development steps for the future.

5. *Action learning.* Participants leave the first-week program in a team that works virtually over the course of six to eight months in what is called a "strategic learning group." The team works on an action learning project with an objective to identify strategic growth opportunities. The results are presented at the end of the second weeklong program to the CEO, chief financial officer (CFO), senior vice president of strategic planning, and the senior vice president of human resources.

Measuring Progress

There are several points in the course of the business year and program cycle for HR to perform various assessments, obtain feedback from participants, and track progress of the program.

- *Talent reviews.* During the talent reviews, new program participants are identified. It is at this time that a diversity assessment can be conducted to determine whether there is a diverse mix of candidates, they are at the appropriate levels, and they provide a good representation of different functions and parts of the business.

- *Gap analysis.* After the external and 360-degree interview assessments have been completed, reviewing the information for development themes provides a good formative evaluation for curriculum content and/or modification to the content. In addition, it can be determined whether improvement is being made in key developmental areas since the organization has an increased focus in those areas.

- *Participation evaluation.* A comprehensive survey is conducted with participants at the end of their two years in the program. The survey covers each element of the program, from assessments to mentoring to coaching and asks participants to evaluate the program from two perspectives: satisfaction and usefulness. Overall, participants have rated their experience in the program a 4.9 on a 5-point scale. They have been most satisfied with the courses, particularly the networking provided. The opportunities for enhancement are in the coaching and mentoring components, because it is largely determined by whom the participant is matched up with in both cases.

- *Progress metrics.* The final area, which is the most important, is looking at the progress of individuals in the program. Over the past several years, physical movement, lateral movement, promotions, and representation in succession plans have been tracked. In the four years since the inception of the program, there have been an average of 23 percent physical moves, 45 percent lateral moves (or expanded roles), and 40 percent promotions. Physical and lateral moves are important because they support growth by moving to different assignment, and in some cases, to a different assignment in a different location, which can help to provide new or different perspectives for an individual. Representation in succession plans is another key metric because it shows that individuals in the program are, in fact, serious candidates for key positions within the organization. In the first three years of the program, the representation of EAD participants in the executive office succession plan went from 44 percent to 61 percent, and it is still improving. This shows a commitment by executives to move to more of a developmental approach to succession planning rather than a replacement approach.

Summary

The EAD program can be viewed as an outstanding organizational intervention to build bench strength. Key success factors were top management support, adequate allocation of resources to the program, and eventually branding and recognition by leadership that this was a key developmental investment for the corporation. Lessons learned include the need to better prepare and develop HR professionals as coaches; and to ensure mentors had the right number of assignments of program participants and could devote time to them. Ultimately, leadership continuity is the critical measure of success of the EAD program, and time will tell if that goal has been met.

Lessons Learned

This case study mentions that the former CEO of Lockheed Martin was responsible for setting his company's goals to include the creation of this succession program. This further reinforces the fact that the CEO is one of the most important variables in the succession function.

The Executive Assessment and Development program, the premier development program for high-potential leaders within Lockheed Martin, sets up a detailed list of criteria for evaluating leadership potential. This company was obviously aware of the importance of assessing all leaders and executives against the same standards.

The EAD program involves two years of both coaching and mentoring for each high-potential executive. This shows the amount of commitment Lockheed Martin has to its talent, as well as the level of time and resource expenditure necessary to ensure thorough development of potential.

The evaluation process under the EAD program is focused on assessing both the program itself and the participants involved. This important factor includes talent reviews, gap analysis, participation evaluation, and progress metrics.

About the Contributor

Marilyn Figlar is the vice president, Leadership and Organizational Development for Lockheed Martin Corporation. In this capacity, she oversees all learning, talent, and leadership development strategies and programs for the corporation. Prior to this role, Marilyn was director, Executive Assessment and Development, and was responsible for talent management, high-potential leadership development programs, and an internal executive coaching program. In other roles with Lockheed Martin, Marilyn served as an organizational effectiveness manager and consultant, developing change strategies and performance improvement interventions. Marilyn has worked as an external consultant, has a BS in psychology and communications from the University of Pittsburgh, an MA in industrial/organizational psychology from Radford University, and is currently completing her dissertation to obtain a PhD in organizational development at Virginia Tech.

7

MERRILL LYNCH

Case Study

Merrill Lynch, one of the world's leading financial management and advisory companies, is a company whose battle to perpetually keep its succession strategy at the top can serve as a model for the implementation of such processes in other industries.

The case study in this chapter outlines the efforts of a particular division—the Global Markets & Investment Banking Group (GMI)—to modify and improve upon a baseline corporate standard. The conflict for this organization arose from the same pressures of the late 1990s mentioned in the previous chapter. GMI's aptitude in dealing with and adapting to changing market conditions, value proposition from employers, and nontraditional competitors has allowed them to turn a previously compliance-driven succession system into a business-focused succession system that became a major driver of how talent was managed in the division.

This chapter highlights no specific conflicts but is unique in the fact that it describes how succession can be tackled on a divisional basis rather than on a whole company scale, showing that it is possible for an individual division to spearhead change. Some notable aspects of this case study are that it provides an excellent look into the necessity of personal discussion in evaluating performance and capability gaps, and provides an accurate look at the level of time commitment necessary for productive individual meetings.

Chapter Outline

Global Markets & Investment Banking Group

Provides an in-depth look into the GMI division of Merrill Lynch, the major player of this case study.

GMI Succession Process

Covers the challenges facing GMI coming out of the 1990s and their business case for a succession system. Also discusses the goals of their endeavor.

Taking Action

Looks at the changes made to the old succession process used by the division.

One-on-One and Talent Review

Looks specifically into the one-on-one talent review sessions practiced by Merrill Lynch, the most important part of the GMI succession program. In addition, looks at yearly changes to the program that display the learning curve of the company, shows evaluation criteria, and provides tangible results.

Lessons Learned

Recaps the important points of the chapter.

The vice president and global head of Executive Leadership for the institutional businesses of Investment Banking, Debt and Equity sales and trading (Corporate and Institutional Client Group or CICG; now called Global Markets & Investment Banking Group) redefined the succession and talent review process of the global business with high impact in talent awareness and key business results. In GMI, they leveraged the corporate process, used strategic dialogues to focus on skill and development, developed key criteria for talent reviews, and leveraged lessons learned to increase the impact year over year.

Merrill Lynch is one of the world's leading financial management and advisory companies, with three core businesses: Global

Private Client, Global Markets & Investment Banking Group, and Merrill Lynch Investment Managers.

Global Markets & Investment Banking Group

The Global Markets & Investment Banking Group is one of the world's top global investment banks, providing institutional sales and trading, investment banking advisory and capital raising services to corporations, governments, and institutions worldwide (see Exhibit 7.1). Building on enduring relationships, they leverage their global resources and market intelligence to deliver innovative, comprehensive solutions to clients.

Global Markets

Global Markets is one of the leading providers of sales and trading services encompassing the full spectrum of debt and equity products for institutional investor clients worldwide. Debt Markets covers interest rate, credit and asset-based products, liability management, foreign exchange, derivatives, and other securities. Their secured financing and principal investing capabilities include commercial and residential real estate. In addition, the group offers a wide range of risk management solutions to clients around the world. Equity Markets provides a full range of equity and equity-linked sales and trading services, including sophisticated portfolio analytics and electronic trading. The group's extensive prime brokerage services

Exhibit 7.1 GMI Snapshot

Countries of operation: 28

Core businesses: Global Markets, Investment Banking, Global Private Equity, Global Leveraged Finance

2004 net revenue: $11,022 million

Source: Merrill Lynch company Web site.

include transaction and portfolio financing, stock lending and clearing, settlement, reporting, and custody.

Global Investment Banking

The Global Investment Banking Group delivers strategic capital-raising and merger and acquisition advisory services with specialized sector expertise. The company's debt and equity origination teams help clients raise funds and diversify capital sources by accessing the domestic, international, and private markets. Corporate finance teams provide superior hedging and structured product solutions tailored to clients looking to maximize returns and minimize risk.

Their global leveraged finance team specializes in high-yield capital markets, loan syndication, and leveraged finance origination.

GMI Succession Process

Historically, the process of succession planning followed two tiers:

1. Corporate Board, chief executive officer (CEO), division level (incorporating succession, talent matrix, high potentials, and state of the business); and
2. Division level (incorporating succession, talent matrix, high potentials, and state of the business)

The process was relatively staid, though it met the overall requirements and needs of the organization; many in GMI looked at the process as one of compliance, and lacking substantial value once completed.

In 2000, GMI created a robust process to significantly raise talent discussions. As a result of the success of this process, leverage was created going into 2001 to continue raising the bar with the management team and to bring it deeper into the organization. The result was a system that enhanced the overall understanding of talent and contributed to the overall enterprise-wide talent reviews.

In the late 1990s, there was an increasing pressure to recruit, develop, and retain talent that was affected by the following factors: market conditions, the value proposition from employers, and nontraditional competitors. There was increasing awareness of the evolving shift of basic demographics: that the supply versus demand of employees was changing based on retiring populations and graduating class sizes, shifting needs and desires of people coming into the workforce, and increasing options for people in the marketplace. As the heady days of the dot-com environment continued, a good deal of talent pursued this space for the excitement and reward opportunity. Additionally, both consulting firms and financial markets firms were pursuing a similar cadre of talent. This was especially true at more junior employee levels, and GMI was losing out on some of the targeted talent to these areas. This brought the focus on recruiting to high awareness in the company. Additionally, as GMI began looking at recruiting issues, the factors around development and retention came into sharper focus: the value proposition a firm could offer included not only traditional compensation components; a company also needed a plan to develop and retain employees. As GMI looked at these factors, focusing on more junior levels of talent at the BA and MBA (analyst and associate) levels, it became clear that these same issues needed to be addressed throughout the organization. And, together all of these factors turned the company's attention to an overarching mechanism in their organizational toolkit: the succession process as a vehicle to address key talent and organizational issues in GMI's platform. In summary, GMI redefined their succession process based on the following factors occurring in the marketplace:

- 1997–1998: McKinsey & Company, a management consulting firm advising leading companies on issues of strategy, organization, technology, and operations, published information on the "war for talent." The recruiting platform was revamped as a result.

- 1999: Recruiting processes were improving and still losing people to dot-coms and nontraditional competitors, so the focus shifted to retention and development efforts.
- 2000: The next logical step was to *focus on talent!*

The following goals were set:

- Leverage the existing process of succession management further/deeper in GMI
- Create a more robust platform by integrating a focus on talent into the succession process
- Focus on strategic issues
- Broaden the Executive Management Committee's understanding of company talent
- "Change the game" of how GMI looked at talent and the succession/talent review process

Taking Action

To accomplish this, the process was reshaped. The old process had the following characteristics:

- One-on-one meeting between the president of GMI and business or region head focused on successors.
- The Executive Management Committee as a group focused on talent matrix and high potentials.
- A limited amount of time was spent, as the process was seen as not productive and more of an enterprise requirement without substantial value to GMI.
- Compounding issues included a heavily matrixed organization and business/regional differences

- Result was confusion, focus on nonessential issues, and not looking deep for bench strength

GMI's new process took steps to keep what was essential and to change the game in the following ways:

- Gave it a new name: GMI Succession Plan 2000: State of Talent Review
- Changed the one-on-one to a targeted discussion (the president of GMI and business/region head and head of Executive Leadership)
- Instituted a talent review process
- Produced a "playbook" for the GMI Executive Management Committee
- Instituted year-end follow-up

The head of executive leadership in GMI worked with the global head of human resources for GMI, global head of training & development for GMI, and the president of GMI in designing the process. Additionally, to ensure compliance with the corporate process, the head of executive leadership served on the enterprise-wide committee for succession planning and talent reviews, and worked with the head of corporate leadership development on the enterprise-wide process, tools, and goals.

At the division level, for GMI, preparing for the one-on-one and talent review process was a global effort across business units and geographies carried out locally by human resource generalists and leadership development professionals. They worked backward from the corporate calendar of deliverables and dates to establish the GMI calendar of deliverables and dates. GMI began with a global kick-off call set by the global head of human resources and led by the head of executive leadership for all HR generalists, training & development, and executive development staff who would be involved in supporting the process in the business to overview how the process would work and answer initial questions. Subsequently, a global meeting or conference call set by the global head of human resources and led by the head of executive leadership was held with the Executive Management Committee on how the process would work and to answer initial questions.

One-on-One and Talent Review

For the one-on-one, a targeted discussion process was implemented. The meeting was held with the president of GMI, the direct report (either live or via video conference), and the head of Executive Leadership. Typical length of the meeting was one hour. The focus was a discussion and review of the status of leadership, business structure, and diversity. Five areas were covered:

1. *Successor pipeline for direct report* (includes people within his or her business line, within GMI, peers on the Executive Management Committee, and people across Merrill Lynch) at immediate and planned levels (immediate could do the job tomorrow, planned was one to three years out, and immediate could also be planned—could do the job, but would be a large stretch; would benefit from additional development).

2. *Talent matrix* (using a 9 box grid looking at performance and potential; see Exhibit 7.2). Performance had three tiers: Inconsistently Achieves, Achieves, and Achieves with Distinction; and Potential also had three tiers: Plateaued, Growth Potential, Highest Potential). Criteria included year-end review ratings, cross-evaluation scores, and compensation.

3. *Highest potentials at each officer level*: managing director, director, and vice president. There was an emphasis on obtaining a diverse list by gender, and for U.S. residents or expatriots race was coded as well. (See Exhibit 7.3.)

4. *Business issues* driving organizational and/or people changes.

5. *Changes in the plan* from the prior year.

Exhibit 7.2 Talent Matrix

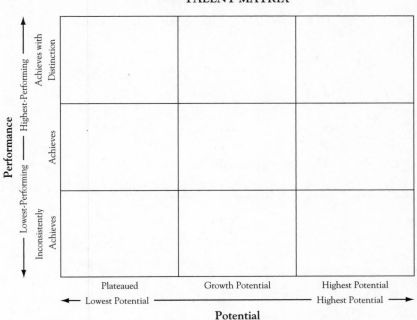

Business Unit/Region Name
TALENT MATRIX

Each year, GMI selected three critical business topics on which to focus the talent review conversations. For instance, in 2000 the topics were

- Key successor to a critical business and/or position
- Someone with cross-border capability (regional or global)
- High potential not well known to the GMI Executive Management Committee

And, in 2001 the topics were

- High potential not well known to the GMI Executive Management Committee
- Diversity (women/minorities)

Exhibit 7.3 Highest Potentials

Business Unit/Region Name
HIGHEST POTENTIALS

Name _____   Business unit _____   Location _____   Diversity Key* _____

*Please include a diverse list and use the following key:

Gender	Race (US residents or expatriots only)
F = Female	A = Asian
M = Male	B = Black, not Hispanic
	H = Hispanic
	I = American an Indian or African
	W = White, not Hispanic

- Skill set of the future (this person should be a *momentum player* capable of a significant move-up in GMI or across the enterprise)

Content required on those identified as high potentials was consistent and included:

- Profile (history at Merrill Lynch/non-ML work, education, unique skills)
- Discussion template (current job, assignments, Critical Few Objectives, accomplishments, strengths, development needs, and future roles)
- Copy of the employee's year-end review
- Copy of his or her cross-evaluation (an online internal review process to gain feedback)

Strategic dialogues were conducted in both the one-on-one and talent review. Since the focus through this process was on approximately 1 percent of the organization, many of the selected employees exhibited the "best of the best" skills: they were highly successful producers, businesspeople, and/or managers. They exhibited the Merrill Lynch principles: client focus, respect for the individual, teamwork, responsible citizenship, and integrity. However, there was also a focus in the discussions on intangibles, including:

- Is the person scalable?
- What is her leadership like?
- Is he fungible—within GMI? Within Merrill Lynch?
- Does she develop/mentor others?
- Does he wear a diversity "headset" effectively?
- What are her relationships in Merrill Lynch—are they only in her group, region, business, or are they across the platform (GMI region, business, and enterprise)?
- What can be learned from his reviews?
- Who on the Executive Management Committee does he *not* know? Who across the enterprise should she meet? What client opportunities does the company want to leverage further?
- What can be learned or leveraged from the person's work history and background?
- What's the best next step for him or her? Why? What is the risk or reward?

From this review process and from in-depth conversations, skill and development needs were identified for each person selected.

GMI spent time to thoughtfully identify key criteria for talent reviews. The obvious: senior management would only take this as a business imperative *if* it addressed business issues. The view was to focus on what was "keeping the Executive Committee members up at night" (or should be), which was termed the "gut-check moment" during the conversation. Key criteria for the GMI Executive Committee member discussions were determined by maintaining a focus on three areas:

1. Involvement with as many facets of the management teams as necessary to understand their business drivers, organizational issues, and structural changes (why/how/impact)

2. Staying abreast of presentations, business plans, industry activity, and macro/micro trends

3. Knowing the GMI Executive Committee member's "pain points" and that change comes from *and* creates impact in these areas

And, a process was integrated to:

• Formulate items and check to ensure fit

• Ensure structure for the reviews (what to prepare and discussion format)

• Create follow-up and accountability so that the review became more than a one-time moment

The result of the talent reviews was that the company was able to summarize what each of the Executive Management Committee members said and produce a single-page document that highlighted the key business issues that GMI faced. In general, all members of the GMI Executive Management committee were aware of the "pain points" of each region and/or business; however, the succession team also wanted to highlight these in a snapshot view and elevate them to the Executive Committee members so that they could collectively consider these issues. GMI had great success addressing organizational challenges as a result of these salient points being collected, shared, and discussed by the team.

In both 2000 and 2001, GMI had approximately 15,000 employees worldwide and a high-potential list of nearly 400 names. Based on the three critical business topics, the target group discussed in detail for the talent reviews was much smaller (35 to 50 people); for these Individuals, development plans were prepared for the coming year.

Much was learned from the process and also helped the process to evolve the next year. Some of the key items learned:

- Tie in competencies more directly.
- Strengthen development plans and accountability by the business heads.
- Leverage at deeper levels in the organization (drill down by business and/or region).
- Have ongoing talent reviews in each business line (What's the same and what's new? Discuss two or three new names to keep the process moving).

The biggest indicator of success during the first year of the process was a fundamental shift in perspective among members of the Executive Management Committee and the human resources community. Although initially, many people felt this only was adding more work/time to the process (going from a traditional meeting of approximately three hours for the "old process" to a commitment in excess of twelve hours of one-on-one meetings, two full days of meetings for the entire Executive Management Committee, plus the additional hours of time and commitment by the human resources community in doing the due diligence and the preparation of each of their respective business and regional heads for the "new process"), following the meetings the president of GMI said that in his fifteen years in the business this was the richest and most complete process he had ever experienced–a comment that was reiterated by all the Executive Management Committee members. Additionally, going into the next year resistance to the change was lower, the process was welcomed, and the time spent in the group meeting was extended. Also, key business issues were addressed, business problems were solved, and talent was surfaced and developed at a higher and more consistent level than had been experienced in the past. As the results of GMI's process were shared at the next level (in Merrill Lynch's CEO's and the president of GMI's one-on-one; and at the firm's management committee meetings), other division heads and their respective leadership development staffs asked them to share more about their process, and parts were integrated into other division processes.

Corporate Snapshot

Founded: 1914 (Charles E. Merrill & Co)
Employees: 50,600
Net Revenue: $US 22 billion
Total Client Assets: $US 1.6 trillion
Assets under Management: $US 501 bn
Total Stockholders' Equity: $US 31.4 bn*
Fortune 500: Ranked No.58
Stock Symbol: MER
Global Markets: 36 countries
As of year-end 2004.

Lessons Learned

• GMI made the decision to modify its succession plan based on several changing market factors: market conditions, the value proposition from employers, and nontraditional competitors. Shifting needs and desires, demographics, and options in the marketplace led to the need for a more efficient process that would give a decisive edge to the company and (more specifically) the GMI department.

• GMI's existing system was modified to greatly extend the one-on-one meetings with formulated and standardized material and agendas. In addition, talent reviews were implemented, allowing for monitoring of key potential; a playbook for planning

*Estimated

goals and strategies was devised; and follow-up sessions were planned in advance.

GMI's new system gives a sense of the amount of time that should be allotted for a successful succession review process. The previous system involved meetings that lasted around an hour; the new system involved one-on-one sessions lasting in excess of twelve hours. Despite the added time commitment, the new program was highly favored among GMI personnel.

About the Contributor

Leigh Fountain is an internationally recognized speaker, coach, facilitator, and author who engages audiences with remarkable results. Leigh is president of Life Force, LLC, a consultancy with a laser focus on teamwork, communication, and leadership. Prior to his work at Life Force, LLC, Leigh built a successful career in Human Resources as both a generalist and specialist with senior executive global roles on Wall Street in institutional sales, leadership, organizational effectiveness, and sales training with Merrill Lynch, Salomon Smith Barney, and Chase Manhattan Bank. Initially working in education, Leigh helped grow a training and organizational consulting business to 275 people. Leigh has academic and clinical training in counseling and coaching and national certification in experiential learning. His master's degree research and thesis was on communication in the workplace. Since 1998 Leigh has served on the faculty of the Global Institute for Leadership Development; since 2003 on the faculty of Best of Organizational Development Summit; and as a faculty member at Tallahassee Community College. Leigh is a founding member of the International Association of Coaches. He is also a contributing author on organizational change in the book *The Art and Practice of Leadership Coaching: 50 Top Executive Coaches Reveal Their Secrets* (John Wiley & Sons, 2005). While at Merrill Lynch, Leigh

Fountain was vice president and global head of executive leadership for the institutional businesses of Investment Banking, Debt and Equity Sales and Trading; and, also, Leigh served as global head of human resources and on the operating committee for Institutional Debt and Equity Sales (Corporate and Institutional Client Group or CICG; now called Global Markets & Investment Banking Group or GMI).

8

RALSTON PURINA PETCARE COMPANY'S CUSTOMER DEVELOPMENT GROUP

Case Study

Purina, a pet food company founded in 1894, has been operating under 100 years of solid tradition. Facing changing market conditions such as globalization, industry consolidation, and e-commerce, the Customer Development Group (CDG), the functional sales division within Purina, was forced to adopt a program that could support a sustainable supply of managers and leaders who were capable of fostering innovation and staying ahead of the competition.

As a 100-year-old company, Purina had a very strong and well-established set of corporate values. The CDG at Purina found a way to successfully work their corporate values into an innovative succession system and use them to its advantage. Using these values and a more open approach to talent development, Purina CDG provides a valuable example of innovative succession strategy.

Chapter Outline

Company Profile
> Describes Purina and its niche within the pet food market.

Customer and Employee Focus
> Discusses the changes facing the market, forcing Purina CDG into adopting new succession methods. Briefly looks at the business case for this initiative.

Business Strategy
> Looks at the underlying values behind the organization and the constraints it had to comply with in the design of its new strategy.

Succession Planning Program Design

Shows the overall plan for the design of the succession process.

The Five Key Philosophies

Describes a set of behavioral models that serve as criteria for potential leaders.

The Planning Process

Displays the key components of the succession system in bullet format, as well as the worksheet format used by both employees and managers to create personal succession plans.

The Performance Appraisal System

Looks at the quarter-year appraisal process under which employees are evaluated.

The Competency Model

Describes the six-point performance scale used to rank employee talent.

Future Utilization or Movement

Discusses the importance of using a transparent process (letting employees know where they stand) and combining that with consistent feedback from potential.

Developmental Interventions

Discusses the differences in training and skill development, two forms of employee progression.

Implementation

Shows the specifics behind the succession plan and how the process itself was implemented.

Evaluation

Looks at employee evaluation and the ways in which employees are assigned training.

Feedback and Analysis

Provides tangible results of the successful program.

Summary

Summarizes the company's reaction to the changes it made and what it learned in the process.

Lessons Learned

Recaps the important points of the chapter.

How does an organization address the departure of key personnel in critical positions, especially when its champions are departing for better job offers. One key solution is to develop a robust succession planning system that includes integration with the existing performance management and strategy planning processes.

This chapter demonstrates how one organization implemented a succession planning process to keep the talent pipeline full and ensure long-term employee and organizational development. As a result of implementing the system, every employee (600-plus) had a succession and supporting personal development plan; the number of succession planning candidates increased from 37 to 179 within the second year of implementation; departures at the top levels decreased to a manageable few, and those who left had "ready-now" successors available to step in; and the organization had a structured and consistent set of criteria and competencies for promotion that could be communicated to current and prospective employees.

Company Profile

At the time of inception of its succession planning program, Purina PetCare Company (subsequently acquired by Nestlé) was a leader in the global pet products industry, with twenty-six manufacturing facilities worldwide. The company's second largest division, after manufacturing, was the Customer Development Group (CDG) with approximately 600 employees. Founded in 1894, Purina has been the leader in pet care for more than 100 years, and their products are found in every shopping format, from mom-and-pop retailers to global sellers like Wal*Mart and Safeway. However, despite having an impressive business history and an extensive list of flagship products, Purina was not without strong competition.

Customer and Employee Focus

At the time Purina had strong competitors in the market, including Friskies (a Nestlé brand, and with the acquisition, now a key Purina brand), Pedigree, Iams, and Science Diet. With intense and successful competitors like these and the pace of change accelerating as globalization, industry consolidation and acquisition, and e-commerce created new markets and new competition, CDG needed to ensure it had managers in place or ready to go who could help increase the organization's capacity for growth, innovation, and long-term sustainability and profitability. New leadership skills would be required to ensure success and to develop the organization's leadership capacity. This goal became a paramount strategic imperative.

Business Strategy

Succession planning was developed and deployed within Purina CDG to help identify and develop world-class leaders and managers who could ensure long-term viability of the company. As a 100-year-old organization, Purina was built on a strong set of values that permeated every facet of the organization, and it was agreed by the CDG management team that this same set of values, which had helped build a strong corporate culture, would be the same set of values that would be integrated into the succession planning system (see Figure 8.1).

Figure 8.1 Purina Values

Stand Tall	*Smile Tall*
Conduct your business affairs with pride and dignity. . . .	Willingly accept challenges with a confidence that no undertaking is too big. . . .
Think Tall	*Live Tall*
Seek innovative solutions to problems. . . .	Do the right things right. . . .

And so, in support of the organization's values and in conjunction with a strategic people imperative, the CDG management team started work to develop and deploy a progressive and robust talent management system that would help to retain current leaders and managers as well as attract new and future high-performing employees. It would be important to get "the right people, with the right skills, in the right place, at the right time, doing the right things" (courtesy of Anne Kurzenberger, organizational effectiveness consultant, 2005).

Succession Planning Program Design

The succession planning system was developed based on benchmarking and research done against the General Electric models available for public consumption as well as the proprietary, members-only material available from the Sales Executive and Corporate Leadership Councils. As word of the succession planning project at CDG went out, employees within the organization shared examples of programs they had been a part of, and as a result, key elements of the program began to emerge. The leadership team agreed that the succession planning process must be aligned with three additional leadership systems:

1. The strategic planning process, during which key organizational initiatives were addressed and timelines for execution set

2. The performance management system, and in particular the personal development planning process, which was built to support development of organizational and leadership competencies and would serve as the supporting mechanism for targeted employee training and development

3. The existing action learning leadership development program, which had been put into place to support leadership competency development while addressing key strategic priorities (see Figure 8.2).

Figure 8.2 The Integrated Leadership System

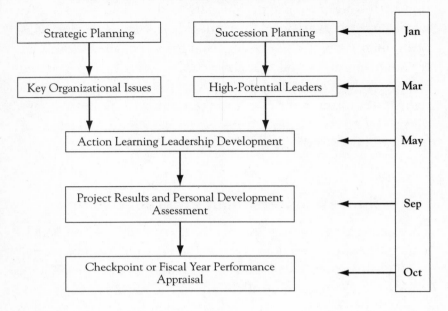

The Five Key Philosophies

The CDG, in support of its decision to create a people-centric culture, had developed five key people philosophies that can be summarized as follows.

1. *Be the best* in everything we say and do and pursue the growth of our "intellectual capital"—our people.

2. *Tell the story.* Build relationships by showing care, compassion, and respect for one another and tell the story of accomplishment to create a legacy of high performance.

3. *Expect to win,* and recognize the importance of family, friends, and colleagues to our success; they help inspire and motivate us to achieve results and deliver beyond expectation.

4. *Create the future* by being flexible. We will be able to quickly mobilize resources to meet the demands of our customers and consumers—seek to create the future by embracing change.

5. *Lead by example* by incorporating these philosophies into your daily actions and interactions.

In order to support these philosophies, management needed to ensure that the succession planning system was viewed as an enabler to building a change-ready organization that would be able to adapt quickly to changing demands by developing and deploying a high-performance leadership group; it could not be seen by employees as an encumbrance to advancement and thus a slow and cumbersome process that ran counter to the espoused values and philosophies.

With these philosophies and values in mind, the leadership team described succession planning as a process for identifying successor candidates who were "ready now" for key leadership positions or who could be ready when specific developmental interventions were completed.

The Planning Process

The purpose of the succession planning process was trifold: (1) to identify employees for development and movement; (2) to contribute to the development of staffing and future recruitment planning; and (3) to ensure that the people development plans were consistent with and supportive of current and future business requirements and needs.

Benefits for the organization and its employees included development of a system that represented a more systematic way to identify candidates for leadership positions, to provide employees with a solid process for career pathing and advancement, and to create a standardized context for leaders to use when reviewing candidates and their readiness for promotion.

Key components that were included in the succession planning process included the following:

- The employee profile, including name, salary grade, position, department, years of service, bonus eligibility, and evaluator's name

- Performance ratings for current and previous years as well as an assessment of potential capabilities
- Leadership behavior ratings or strengths against key competencies, which included business domain as well as people leadership competencies and developmental opportunities (which could include assignment to a training or developmental intervention)
- Noteworthy professional experiences or skills, which included certifications, licenses, or specialized programs completed by the employee and relevant to the business
- Education level achieved, including the degree obtained, the university attended, and the year the degree was obtained
- Key contributions made during the current year of service, focusing on the top two or three achievements
- Future utilization and possible next moves, including short- and long-term potential, the employee's willingness to relocate, and to which geographic locations
- Top two potential successors, including those who were ready now to move as well as those ready soon for a move
- Languages spoken, which provided employees' recognition for fluency in languages other than English (important information should candidates be considered for an international role)
- Work history, including the past three organizations and job titles

All of this information was integrated onto a one-page worksheet and completed for every employee in the CDG (see Exhibit 8.1). All employees completed a personal succession plan using the same document as their manager. The manager then integrated the employee's feedback into his or her form, which was used as the final form in the succession planning discussions. Most of the successions planning components are self-explanatory; the few exceptions warrant additional definition.

Exhibit 8.1 CDG's Individual Succession Planning Worksheet

Individual Review for Employee Succession Planning

Name: Salary Grade:
Position: Evaluator:
Department: Current Date:
Years of Service: Bonus Plan:

Category	Rating		Key Strengths (Limit to top 3)	Development Priorities (Limit to top 3)
	Last Yr.	Current Yr.	1.	1.
Performance			2.	2.
Potential			3.	3.

BRIEFLY Describe Top 3 Key Contributions/Accomplishments (Limit to 1 or 2 sentences per item):
1.
2.
3.

Potential Next Move(s)	Dept.	Readiness	Comments

Potential Successor(s)	Readiness	Comments

Educational Attainment

Degree/Major	School	Year Attained

Other Noteworthy Professional Experiences/Skills:

Willingness to Relocate (Select all that apply):

_____ Not Mobile
_____ Temporarily Not Mobile
_____ Domestic Mobility
_____ International Mobility

Native Language: **Other Language(s) also fluent in:**

PREVIOUS Professional Work History (last 5 years):

Start Date (00/00/00)	End Date (00/00/00)	Job Title	Company Name (if not RPCO)

Miscellaneous Comments:

The Performance Appraisal System

The performance appraisal system within the CDG was comprised of a five-point rating scale; each employee was provided directional feedback on a quarterly basis with formal assessment occurring annually. The scale is presented in Table 8.1. Knowledge of an employee's performance rating was important in succession planning for two reasons: it enabled universal understanding of the performance rating for that candidate, and only employees with a 4 or 5 rating—or an employee identified as a top-performing 3—were included in the succession planning process. This meant that on average, the management team would be evaluating close to 200 candidates a year.

Current and previous years' performance ratings were integrated as a mechanism for assessing continued and assumed performance potential of the candidate for the upcoming year and/or in a new role. An employee who was rated a 5 two years in a row was more likely to be identified as a ready-now candidate, all other components considered, than a ready-soon candidate.

Table 8.1 The Performance Rating Scale

5	Significantly Exceeds Expectation: Outstanding performance; clearly exceeded requirements in all key areas
4	Exceeds Expectation: Superior performance; fully met and frequently exceeded requirements in all key areas
3	Meets Expectation: Competent performance; met and sometimes exceeded expectation
2	Meets Some Expectations: Improvement needed; some good work accomplished, but improvement needed to meet normal job requirements
1	Does Not Meet Expectations: Unsatisfactory performance; results below expectation, performance improvement plan (PIP) required
M	Missing: Cannot assess due to lack of information

The Competency Model

In CDG, managers were assessed against two competency areas: functional or domain specific competencies and general management competencies. A skill assessment was also conducted against key skills deemed essential to success. Competency and skill assessments could be derived from two sources: the employee's 360-degree feedback report or from employee self-assessment (for new employees who had not yet participated in 360 feedback) and direct supervisor input. Competency assessment was based on a six-point scale:

1. *Definitely exceptional*. Employee embodies the behavior or skill and is considered a role model for others.

2. *Clear strength*. Employee exhibits obvious and definite proficiency with respect to behavior or skill.

3. *Solid performer*. Employee performs at a level consistent with expectation; he or she does not excel, nor requires remediation.

4. *Opportunity for improvement*. Employee is in need of development and is motivated to change.

5. *Critical need*. Employee has an obvious and critical need for change in this behavior or skill.

6. *Missing*. Employee cannot be assessed due to lack of information, knowledge, or observable behavior or may be too new to adequately assess.

The competency and skill assessment was important in determining what type of developmental intervention or job experience the candidate should be exposed to and/or assigned to complete. Thus a manager with a need for development of several general manager competencies as well as skill development in areas such as coaching and team building could be assigned to participate in the action learning leadership development program, while a candidate with top rating in all three areas could be placed in the ready-now successor pool for promotional consideration.

Future Utilization or Movement

Employees' feedback on their availability to relocate was important because it could impact their ability to move and/or be promoted to the next level. It was important to obtain this information upfront from employees, but also to communicate the potential next move upon completion of the succession planning process, so that the employee knew exactly where he or she stood relative to future movement and promotion.

Developmental Interventions

The succession planning process was supported by a list of training and developmental interventions. Training was considered appropriate if immediate skill enhancement was needed. Training could include programs such as financial analysis, sales skills, problem-solving skills and tools, and performance coaching. Developmental interventions were considered appropriate if the employee was deemed to be ready soon and the management team wanted to expose him or her to a more robust and complex project in preparation for the next role. They were considered appropriate for longer-term career development and growth and could be part of a system of interventions required for movement. Programs such as special assignments or job rotation, process improvement projects, action learning, and team development were considered developmental in nature and generally were assigned when an employee needed competency development in the general manager or domain specific competencies.

A key and noteworthy feature of the succession planning process was that it was not a closed-door process. The Individual Succession Planning Worksheet (presented earlier as Exhibit 8.1) was available to employees online, and their feedback was solicited annually prior to the management assessment process. Employees were aware of the timeline for all people processes (for example, the performance management cycle, the succession planning

Figure 8.3 Key People Process Timeline

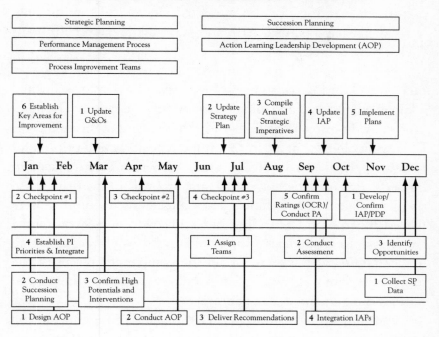

cycle, the leadership development program dates, and so on). In addition, because of the timing, results of the succession planning discussion were shared with employees in conjunction with the annual performance assessment process, and critical training or developmental interventions (for example, process improvement teams and action learning) were aligned to enable speed in competency development, if selected as the appropriate activity (see Figure 8.3).

Implementation

End of year for Purina is in October. As such, key processes such as performance management and succession planning were aligned accordingly. Data collection for succession planning followed the year-end performance appraisal process so that performance ratings for the previous year and upcoming year, individual action plans (IAP), and personal development plans (PDP) were complete.

Succession planning meetings generally occurred in a cascaded process and during the month of January. The employees would complete their forms and submit them to their managers. The manager would in turn complete his or her assessment of the employee. Data was collected in a central online repository and printed for review by the leadership team. Employees' forms were placed in binders based on geography and team, and within the team based on role and performance rating. Thus, all sales representatives were placed together in ascending order by performance rating for the region. Regional leadership would review employees to ensure understanding and agreement on the component pieces of the form. This data was then updated and saved back in the central repository.

The senior leadership team (senior vice president and top five direct reports, as well as a representative from Organizational Effectiveness) would meet for two days and review the top-rated employees (for example, top-performing 3s and all 4s and 5s). This meeting was conducted off-site and away from the workplace to ensure confidentiality of information and materials.

The top positions (for example, managing directors) were reviewed and key assessment made on the next probable career move and top two developmental interventions. Successors for the managing director (MD) role were sorted by top five "ready within one move" and top five "ready within two moves." The organization had previously identified a need for developing a more diverse group of leaders at the top, so an eye was kept on the state of minority and female candidates. In some cases, their development was accelerated to ensure they were capable of movement sooner versus later.

The remaining candidates were sorted by succession plan form and potential for succession to managing director (next one or two moves), directors next, team leaders third, and then all other key personnel or positions.

All candidates were assessed by group against domain and general manager competencies and skills, previous or current work experience and knowledge, movement and promotability potential, performance rating average, and other (for example, education, interests and hobbies, developmental intervention priority). A grid (see Exhibit 8.2) was produced for assessment of candidates within each grouping, including current and potential successors (for example, MD, director-sales, director-multifunctional role, team leader, and other key people or positions). This information in turn was used to determine recommended career paths or movement for key roles and/or individuals. For example, a minority team leader was mapped against current requirements (competency, skills, and job experience required) for movement into a MD role. Thus the leadership team utilized their knowledge of what it took to be a successful managing director based on succession planning experience and mapped out all of the work experience, training, and/or developmental intervention the individual would need and plotted that person's career path accordingly.

While all employees included in the succession planning discussion were provided with feedback on potential next role and development requirements, only a few (for example, minority, female, or level 5 performers) received feedback relative to their career planning "map." The top fifty employees rated by the CDG were identified for review at the corporate leadership level. At the time, the CDG had the most robust and uniform succession planning process; it later became the company standard, and all forms and instructions were put online for ease of access, completion, and compilation.

Exhibit 8.2 Purina's Succession Planning Group Summary

Competency, Skills, Knowledge Scale—DE, CS, S, O, CN, M

Name												
Functional Competencies												
Customer Relationship Mgmt												
Sales Management												
Accounting and Financial Management												
Supply Chain and Logistics												
General Leadership												
General Manager Competencies												
Results Driven, Focused												
Emotional Intelligence												
Highly Trusted												
Conceptual Thinker												
Systems Thinker												
Personal Courage												
Skills												
Coaching/Mentoring												
Managing Change												
Developmental Intervention												
Communication												
Negotiation												
Problem Solving												
Team Building												
Summary of Competencies and Skills												

Exhibit 8.2 (*Continued*)

Name													
Experience/Knowledge (X in box)													
General Management (Multi-Function)													
Finance													
Supply Chain/Manufacturing													
Sales and Marketing													
Strategic Planning/Integration													
Knowledge Application													
Human Capital/Human Resources													
Organizational Design/Change Management													
International													
IS/Engineering/R&D													
Movement & Promotability													
Relocatable (Y/N/DN)													
Utilization Short Term (12 mo)													
Utilization Long Term (12–36 mo.)													
Utilization Cross Functionally (Area)													
Next Probable Career Move (Name)													
Other													
Formal Education (List highest level)													
Interests/Hobbies, if Appropriate													
Development Intervention Priority													
Performance Rating Trend													
Average Perf. Rating Over Two-year Period													

Evaluation

The path to development of an effective succession planning process was not without challenges. The first year, the leadership team attempted to assess every employee and found the process overwhelming. Subsequent evaluations were conducted only for the top-performing employees identified by their performance ratings (for example, top 3s, 4s, and 5s). The leadership team learned it was easy to assess individuals by category and like roles versus by region or team. Thus all MDs were evaluated together; the four categories of directors were assessed together based on category, as were team leaders. From this assessment, a list of employees ready now or ready soon for the top positions could be prepared. Drilling down from managing director to key positions also helped ensure consistency and thoroughness of the review.

In the first year of the process, employees were reviewed strictly against the domain competencies. This did not provide the leadership team with enough information about general management competencies and skills, which were being utilized for leadership development in the 360-degree assessment, personal development planning, and action learning processes. It was decided to include this information to ensure a more thorough assessment of overall leadership capability.

Simpler issues were brought to light that helped improve the process, such as alphabetizing and numbering the pages with the succession planning repository and grouping employees by role versus by region for ease of comparative assessment. A "cheat sheet" of competency and rating definitions was provided to ensure that every leader in the succession planning meeting had a universally agreed-upon definition of the components being rated and could refer to it if needed during the meeting. A list of agreed-upon developmental interventions was identified and utilized to ensure consistency in development and training opportunities for all associates. As a side note, this also helped ensure that the programs delivered against the developmental and business needs of CDG. Table 8.2

Table 8.2 CDG Developmental Interventions

Internal Activities	External Programs*
• Participate in a customer-related activity: Account Call, Business Planning, CSI Action Planning, Top-to-Top presentation • Participate in "work-withs" in other functions to develop a broader systems perspective: Marketing, IM, ORM, Product Supply, Plants, Trade Development, Industry Development, Trade Shows, Consumer Events, OCA, Associate Company • Participate in or lead special projects, work assignments, or task forces • Lead or moderate any CDG or ULC training program • Participate in formal job rotation (generally done in preparation for a leadership role) • Obtain external coaching • Seek out a formal mentoring relationship • Formally mentor other associate(s) • Attend specific leadership development programs (refer to list in External Programs column) • Attend a minority or women's leadership conference or recruiting forum to grow diversity awareness • Lead or facilitate a large group or team meeting • Create a personal vision, brand, and action plan; then work your personal brand plan • Develop and work your organizational and external network.	**Minority/Women Leadership Programs** • The African-American Leadership Program (CCL or UCLA) • The Women's Leadership Program (CCL or UCLA) • Women in Leadership Summit (Linkage/February) • Diversity Conference (Linkage/March) • Black MBA Conference • Hispanic MBA Conference • SIFE Competition **Leadership Development** • AOP Action Learning (CDG/April) • Foundations of Leadership (CCL) • Leadership Development Program (CCL) • Teams Conference (Linkage) **Advanced Topics in Leadership** • Emerging Leader Program (Linkage/October) • Developing the Strategic Leader (CCL) • Leadership and High Performance Teams (CCL) **Sales Management** • Penn State, Michigan State, ASU Supply Chain **Customer Relationship Management** • USC Food Retailing Institute • Cornell Food Retailing Institute • SJU Specific Programs (Contact Paul Converse) CCL: Center for Creative Leadership (www.ccl.org)

*These programs range in price from $1,500 to $10,000 per associate and may not reflect the full compliment of programs available to associates through external sources. It does reflect a listing of known external programs with which the organization has a known and positive experience. Please contact Organizational Effectiveness for additional information and dates.

Table 8.3 Developmental Intervention List (Sample)

Name	Next Probable Career Move	Developmental Intervention (Top 1–2 for each person. Use DI list)
		1
		2

provides a sample of the types of developmental interventions available to employees within CDG. Developmental activities helped to build and grow more than one competency or skill area. As such, an employee in need of both skill and general manager competency or experience/knowledge development could be assigned to only one developmental intervention, such as action learning.

Developmental interventions were used in personal development planning discussions to ensure the employee was on track to participate in the program and aware that he or she might be assigned to a particular project or job rotation. The information was also provided to the Organizational Effectiveness team to ensure that employees were enrolled in the appropriate workshop or program. See Table 8.3.

Feedback and Analysis

The succession planning process within the Customer Development Group evolved and improved over time as a result of two elements. The first was an anecdotal assessment of the process by the Organizational Effectiveness director immediately following the meeting. Improvements noted were based on the effectiveness of the process or aspects that caused lengthy debate to occur. For example, when the issue of diversity development was highlighted and accelerated career pathing was undertaken, it became evident that sales leadership roles (such as managing director) required a breadth of experience with differing customers, types of teams, in the retail environment, and sales representative experience. This path became the "gold" process for all employees seeking to pursue a career in sales management.

Additional metrics included an assessment of movement and promotion. Because Purina was an advocate for people development and CDG in particular supported development of a people-centric culture, it was important that employees feel that movement was possible and that developmental interventions and training programs were available to facilitate that process. The training and development budget for the organizational was approximately $2 million.

As a result of focusing on succession planning and the integration of development with other systems, such as action learning leadership development, within three years of implementation (1999–2001) CDG had achieved the following business results:

- Improved from number 15 in an industry customer satisfaction survey to number 1
- Maintained and grew volume and market share numbers in a flat economy and despite intense competitive pressures
- Created leadership bench strength that goes three layers deep
- Reached more than fifteen promotions or new assignments annually
- Improved longevity of leadership positions, enabling uninterrupted and consistent focus on the business
- Created an intensive process for developmental interventions through resolution of real-time issues that represent critical opportunities for the company
- Was able to speak honestly and candidly about the robustness of the succession planning process and the opportunities available to new hires and potential recruits at both employee orientation as well as recruiting events

Summary

Succession planning is most successful when it is top-down driven and strategically and systemically aligned to support or be supported by other human resource or people systems.

Three factors produced an effective process within the CDG at Purina:

1. The leadership team dedicated time and effort to the process and utilized it as the method for promotion.

2. The culture of the organization supported the concept of self-development and career planning. Thus, when succession planning was deployed, it was made available to all employees; although not all employees were reviewed and assessed by the seniormost management team, every employee received feedback on his or her career potential and requirements via the performance management process and personal development plan.

3. The system was mainly support by two company directors: the Quality director who helped to formulate and design the process steps and forms and the Organizational Effectiveness director, who facilitated the succession planning meeting, summarized data, and drove many of the supporting processes, such as performance management, leadership development, developmental activities, mentoring, and 360-degree competency assessment, to ensure integration of the total system.

The system developed in the CDG was so successful it later became the process utilized throughout the organization and, when the company was acquired by Nestlé, information on top-performing employees and career potential was available for use by the human resource planning team.

The strategic imperative for the CDG was to develop a process to keep top performers from defecting from the company and to attract new high potentials to the company. As James White, then vice president of Customer Development said, "Businesses don't compete, people do. It's about who can put the best team of players on the field to win."

Lessons Learned

- To understand the significance of CDG's endeavor to adopt a new and up-to-date succession program, one must realize that this is a company that has been around for more than 100 years. The company was able to readily adapt to increasing competition and changing market conditions such as globalization, retailer industry consolidation, and improving e-commerce.

- One outstanding aspect of this company is their genuine commitment to individuals. Employees were actively involved in the creating of the succession program through relevant advice and sharing of experiences with other companies.

- Once again reflecting CDG's focus on the individual, employees are required to fill out a succession form on themselves (the same form used by managers); that form is then used in conjunction with the manager's appraisal to make a final employee profile.

- Three additional leadership systems accompany the succession process: The strategic planning process, the performance management system, and the action learning leadership development program.

- When reviewing employee profiles, CDG seems to delve deep into specifics. The notable characteristics of their employee assessments are that they place legitimate consideration into previous ratings with the company and extra languages spoken.

- As with most (if not all) successful succession programs, CDG's was a completely transparent process. Employees were continually kept up to date on their positions within the group, their perceived potential, possible future career moves, and development opportunities.

- The succession program used by CDG was extremely deep and involved everything from employee scouting and appraisal, performance and potential mapping, goal setting, development, retention, and training.

About the Contributors

Janice Duis is an organizational effectiveness consultant with more than eighteen years of experience in human resource development and organizational effectiveness. Her expertise is in personal agency, action learning, and change leadership. She has worked in a variety of industries including travel, insurance, retail, consumer package goods, education, and health care. Having been on the business side of the table, she approaches her work with a keen awareness of the business requirements and metrics and aligns interventions to support systemic and whole system change. She was formerly the director of Organizational Effectiveness for the Customer Development Group at Ralston Purina PetCare Company. Prior to joining Safeway Consumer Brands as the Director of Strategy and Business Process, she ran her own consulting company, Authentic Pathways. You can reach her at janice.duis@safeway.com for additional information about her work and this chapter.

James White is the senior vice president of Corporate Brands at Safeway Company. He is a progressive leader and has successfully led in Fortune 500 companies such as Coca-Cola, Nestlé Purina PetCare, the Gillette Company, and Safeway. He is a strategic thinker and focuses on the development of people as a key strategy for growth. He is responsible for the positive results and financial success of every organization he has led. His focus has always been on the development of people and implementation of forward-thinking processes to drive performance. James is presently driving results within his new assignment at Safeway.

9

UNILEVER

Case Study

> People are the heart of our business. Harnessing,
> developing and rewarding skills, energy and
> commitment is our priority.
> —*From Unilever's Corporate Purpose*

Unilever is one of the world's most successful consumer goods companies, with trusted brands in home, personal care, and food products across the globe. Their brand portfolio includes world favorites such as Lux, Dove, Pond's, Lipton, and Knorr, and also regional products and local varieties of famous-name goods. Their reputation as one of the world's most admired employers has been achieved by the company offering opportunities for their people to pursue their goals, both professionally and personally. And because Unilever operates a truly global business, they value the importance of diversity and differences in their workforce for delivering outstanding results. Their work ethic extends to and pervades all their businesses throughout the world, not least Unilever Indonesia (ULI), which has consistently been ranked one of the best-performing companies in operating profits and revenue in the Unilever world, and is also recognized as one of the best in building an enterprise culture.

However, with competition "hotting" up both from multinational and local companies, and with ULI setting its sights on doubling its business from US$1 billion to US$2 billion in the next five years, having a succession planning system that will enable ULI to overcome the tough challenges ahead is absolutely crucial. This chapter thus describes how ULI has built and implemented a strong and robust succession planning system adapted from global initiatives to flourish in their local context, which they hope will drive their five-year business vision toward fruition. As with many large global multinationals, talent management initiatives tend to be corporate-driven ones prescribed by the head office. However, while many of the succession planning initiatives described in this case study may be worldwide initiatives, the discipline with which these initiatives are executed at ULI is what has made the difference, and what has made them so successful.

At ULI, succession planning is not so much a stand-alone initiative or program targeted merely to identify a pool of talent for effective resource deployment.

Succession planning is not one part of talent management—it *is* the entire talent management. It is looked at holistically and woven into the recruitment, selection, appraisal, and development processes of the organization. All these provide the necessary components for identifying future talent and having a well-managed pool of resources to pick from at any given time. The following are the succession planning levers that ensure that the system is a functional and robust one:

- Management Trainee (MT) program
- Mid-Career Recruits (MCR) program
- Performance development plan (PDP)
- Divisional Balanced Business Plan (BBP) (Balanced Scorecard)
- Human Resource (HR) planning sessions
    —Talent review
    —Forced ranking
    —Succession pipeline
    —New appointments
    —Organization structure
- Top succession

- Talent development
  —Coaching and mentoring
  —Career counseling
  —Leadership development

The foundation upon which these succession planning levers are built is a competency and skills-based approach that entails the strengthening and improvement of a set of competencies and functional skills that is deemed necessary for the job of the incumbent, and/or that he or she already possesses. The whole mechanism is geared toward the creation of broad as well as functional talent pools to meet the operational requirements of the business, not only to the benefit of the organization, but also to the incumbent in the wide spectrum of career opportunities available to him or her. This case study thus examines all the different initiatives that make up the succession planning system at ULI, and how they work together to ensure that its succession and talent pipeline is continuously being filled and replenished with the best talents available to meet and exceed consumer needs in the Indonesian market, and drive outstanding business results.

Chapter Outline

Introduction
Provides an overview of the company and the ULI branch.

Business Strategy
Looks at the business case for having a structured and well-defined succession strategy.

Employee Focus
Discusses how the needs of the employee are aligned with the needs of the company, introduces the performance development plan and Balanced Business Plan concepts.

Design and Implementation
Outlines Unilever's philosophy on employee development. Contains sections on Management Trainee program,

Mid-Career Recruits program, strengthening competencies and skills, performance development program, Balanced Business Plan, HR planning sessions, forced ranking, top succession, talent development, key leadership development initiatives, and the Generative Coaching Model.

Feedback and Analysis

Looks at the yearly review program and how changes are made to the new succession system.

Evaluation

Discusses the ways in which the ULI succession system is evaluated.

Lessons Learned

Lists the most important points of the study.

Introduction

> Our long-term success requires a total commitment
> to exceptional standards of performance and
> productivity, to working together effectively, and to
> a willingness to embrace new ideas and learn
> continuously.
> —*From Unilever's Corporate Purpose*

Although Unilever wasn't formed until 1930, the two companies that joined forces to create the business were already well established before the start of the twentieth century: Margarine Unie (Netherlands) and Lever Brothers (United Kingdom). Unilever is now one of the world's leading suppliers of fast-moving consumer goods, with 400 brands spanning fourteen categories of home, personal care, and food products. The Unilever mission is to "add vitality to life and meet the everyday needs for nutrition, hygiene, and personal care with brands that help people feel good, look good and get more out of life." Today, Unilever has businesses in more than 100 countries with 234,000 employees worldwide.

Unilever Indonesia (ULI) was formed in 1933 and is strongly integrated into the local and regional economies. In 2000, ULI directly employed approximately 2,500 people, with an additional 20,000 people engaged in activities through different partnerships. More than 1,200 companies, many of them small- or medium-sized enterprises (SMEs), distribute their products or supply raw materials and packaging to ULI. In recognition of its impact on SMEs, the government presented the company with the prestigious Upakarti Award in 1988, the highest award for corporate contributions in the development of SMEs.

ULI and the rest of the company have always been firm believers in community development and sustainability projects to benefit others. In fact, the entire Unilever family believes that the very business of "doing business" in a responsible way has a positive social impact. They create and share wealth and knowledge, invest in local economies, and develop people's skills—both inside the organization and in the communities. Vitality clearly defines what they stand for: their values, what makes them different, and how they contribute to society.

Business Strategy

Unilever strongly believes that their people are fundamental to the way they do business and are at the center of everything they do. This culture is so strongly ingrained throughout the group that if you speak to any Unilever employee from any country or business unit, he or she will most likely tell you that Unilever is thought of more as a community or family than as an organization.

The natural outflow of this strong people-centered culture means succession planning is not a "nice-to-have" but a "need-to have" and "need-to-win." It is part of a business strategy that asserts that in order to grow the business, you must first grow the people. In fact, "we grow as a company by growing our people" is not a lifeless mantra but a deeply held belief and a truly espoused value. All efforts are aligned with this belief, and everything is done in Unilever's power to find and develop the right people and keep them fulfilled and committed in order to grow the business.

Overall Business Case

The business case for having a well-structured and effective succession planning system in ULI is clear.

- In the current climate of increased competition and growing demands from customers and consumers, it is vital to ensure that the right talent is identified and lined up for the right positions at any time needed to deliver the best possible results in the shortest possible time—not only at top management levels—to keep the leadership pipeline filled, but also for key positions throughout the organization.
- The war for talent continues to make its presence felt, and it is clear that today's generation of employees are looking beyond financial rewards when making the decision to join or stay with a company. Clearly articulated development plans, career roadmaps, and broadened opportunities fuel the attraction and retention of key talent crucial to the sustained operations and performance of the organization.
- The new and leaner leadership and organization structure means that there is now an ideal platform and framework within which the succession planning system is able to flourish to meet the following business goals for increased revenue and profits:

  - Faster growth
  - Consumer and shopper integration
  - Customer management
  - Speed and simplification
  - Lower cost

- To deal with the challenges of a global marketplace, having a diverse talent pool feeding into the succession pipeline is critical.

It ensures a continual rejuvenation of mindsets, keeps the organizational soil fertile for new and innovative ideas, and keeps the organization in touch with consumer trends and needs to stay ahead of or overtake the competition.

Employee Focus

If the succession planning system in ULI were viewed as a linear or cyclical process, then the start of that process would be the employee. The design of the entire succession planning system hinges first on the individual's career aspirations and motivations, which then feed into his or her performance development plan (PDP) (see section on "Performance Development Plan" later in the chapter for more details). This, of course, does not exist in an arbitrary vacuum but is aligned with the organization's needs. Each division has a balanced scorecard called the Balanced Business Plan (BBP), which also addresses both people and organization needs (see section on "Balanced Business Plan" for more details).

In essence, the PDP and BBP are launching pads for all the other aspects of succession planning, with the exception of the Management Trainee and Mid-Career Recruits programs, which are the preliminary inputs into the system (see Figure 9.1). That is, the succession planning process starts the moment recruitment of talent takes place, since recruitment provides the organization with the necessary resources (human capital) it needs for the creation of talent pools. Another way of looking at it is that recruitment

Figure 9.1 Unilever Indonesia's Succession Planning System

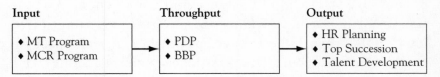

Input	Throughput	Output
♦ MT Program ♦ MCR Program	♦ PDP ♦ BBP	♦ HR Planning ♦ Top Succession ♦ Talent Development

Note: This is not an official Unilever or Unilever Indonesia succession planning design or model. It is for illustrative purposes only.

supplies the "raw materials" for succession planning, while the PDP and BBP serve as the "testing ground" to assess the quality of the materials (in this case, employee needs and competencies), from which to launch the succession planning process proper (that is, the output of succession planning).

Therefore, employee needs are assessed in the design of the succession planning system primarily via the "throughput" channel as shown in Figure 9.1. Where employee needs are met, however, is primarily via the "output" factors. For example, employees' needs may be met by a range of talent development initiatives such as leadership development workshops, executive or peer coaching, mentoring, or career counseling. Should it be the case that any one component of the succession planning system does not address employees' needs in some form directly or indirectly, the imbalance between meeting individual and organizational needs would eventually result in the system becoming obsolete, as it would not be able to withstand the employee apathy, indifference, or dissatisfaction arising from what would be perceived as a lackluster career roadmap.

Design and Implementation

There were two critical success factors that ULI looked at while designing their succession planning system. To evaluate and deem the system successful, system designers had to fulfill these two extremely important criteria: (1) having the right people in the right place at any time needed; and (2) having diversity of "corporate talent" in their talent pool.

What "having a pool of corporate talent" means is that ULI talents have first to be fully assessed for their potential in multifunctional areas by providing them varied opportunities to broaden the scope of their careers, before they are seen to belong to a specific functional talent pool (for example, marketing). ULI starts with the mindset that the talent pool is a corporate one, or rather, that the incumbent is first a corporate or generic talent before she becomes a functional expert (that is, one tied to a specific function such as marketing, audit, accounting, human resources, and so on). This would especially apply to the management trainees when they are recruited into the MT program. However, ULI also keeps an open mind so as to accommodate others who may, for example, have grown up in the company pursuing one career track and who subsequently wish to explore a different one or switch careers midway. ULI believes that opportunity should be given to its people to try on a variety of roles as part of their development plan.

The two success factors anchoring the succession planning system in ULI are highly interdependent and mutually reinforcing. While conventional wisdom may tell you that matching a university degree to a job, or confining and growing a specialist in his field of expertise, will extract the most value out of the system for the good of the business, it doesn't give any room to seek out latent strengths, hidden talents, and genuine rather than superficial job fits, which may otherwise be a tremendous asset to the organization. If there is no diversity in the talent pool to begin with, it can hardly be convincing that the right people are being placed in the right jobs. And if you don't believe you have recruited the best talents or that the ideal job didn't exist for your talent, then building a diverse corporate talent pool would hardly serve any real purpose.

The real money question is this: Are you able to fill any vacancy at any time, in an acceptably short time frame because you have already identified who the highly promising candidates are and planned for the likely successors in advance? In ULI's case, an acceptably short time frame to fill a position would be around one month. If the answer is no, then, as they say, it's "back to the drawing board." This is the standard that ULI places on themselves to ensure that they are continually managing and utilizing their talents in the most effective manner possible, and that there are a dearth of leaders coming down the leadership and succession pipelines to meet the ever-changing needs of the business.

The Management Trainee Program

The MT program was started at ULI in the early 1970s. Even in those early years, a pipeline had been put in place. Most of the top management team members and about 70 percent of the executives belonging to the next level down were all management trained. The concept of the MT program is to recruit for the brightest and the best first without consideration for the type of academic background or work experience of the incumbent. Strictly speaking, the criteria for recruitment into the MT program consist of excellent academic record, excellent interpersonal skills, being motivated, and the ability to perform under pressure. For example, just because an incumbent has an accounting background or degree does not automatically position her for an accounting role in the organization. It is the purpose of the MT program to draw out the strengths and capabilities of each individual during his or her journey at Unilever, especially in the first year.

Once recruited, employees go through a one-year orientation program that exposes them to the different parts of the organization and gives them a thorough evaluation of their strong suits and performance. Recommendations by line managers and HR are then made on where best to place the individuals. Because of the willingness of the organization to take the time and effort to seek out and utilize the best of their management trainees' abilities in line with their passions and interests, a powerful win-win dynamic is usually the outcome. It may sound like a simple and straightforward process, able to reap countless benefits for the organization, but truth be told, it takes commitment and patience to carry through this counter-conventional approach. How many organizations are able to say that their flight engineer turned into an accountant? And would they even want to? Or for their marketing manager to become a corporate learning manager? At ULI, these cases are real and not uncommon.

The basis of this approach stems from the ability to take a long-term view of people's potential. This can take several forms:

1. Assessing the incumbent's current performance and predicting what his potential is in the future

2. Treating the incumbent as corporate talent and continually exploring any hidden capabilities that could add greater value to other parts of the organization than the one currently assigned

3. Suspending judgment on the incumbent's potential until such time that the organization wants to take a calculated risk and give her the opportunity to take on a larger stretch role or assignment

The Mid-Career Recruits Program

The help of external headhunters is enlisted for the recruitment of mid-career hires at ULI. While it is common practice to employ mid-career hires in many organizations, ULI pays special attention to them. This is why the dedicated MCR program was created to address the very specific strategic needs of the organization. Unlike many organizations, the hiring of MCRs at ULI is not seen as a "last resort" to be used when in-house talent is unavailable. The MCR program is part of the broader organizational and people strategy and has several specific roles designed for it:

1. To provide much-needed expertise in the areas that in-house talent is unable to, for example, when a new business is acquired

2. To ensure diversity and avoid stagnation and inbreeding in the workplace, to encourage continual rejuvenation of mind-sets, and to keep the organizational soil fertile for new and innovative ideas to stay ahead of or overtake the competition

3. To expand the existing base of competencies and skill sets of employees

To counter any negative perceptions of MCRs in a community-like environment in which the majority are long-serving staff, effort is made to communicate to all staff that MCRs will not take their jobs and are not a threat to them. Furthermore, ULI has a "buddy" program, which was introduced in 1999, that helps the MCR integrate into the organization and team smoothly within the shortest possible time by appointing a "buddy" to the new person. Usually, the buddy is appointed from a different division.

The program gained greater significance when the company was hit by a talent crisis in 1999 and ULI reorganized to aim for challenging growth. The newly created Corporate Relation division and the expansion of the business into new categories required them to look for new talents outside the company. As an indication of the success of the program today, the retention of MCRs typically stands at a relatively high rate of 76 percent.

Strengthening Competencies and Skills

Before one can look at the design and implementation of the other components within the succession planning system at ULI, one must first understand the competency and skills-based approach that lies at the heart of all the development processes in the organization. First, how does ULI define competencies? *Competencies* are the qualities that allow exceptional leaders to deliver growth at all levels of the business. Leadership is defined by behavior, not by hierarchy. ULI's competency model, called the Leadership Growth Profile (LGP), is therefore applied to all management levels starting from assistant managers. It is relevant not only to those who have direct responsibility for individuals or teams, but also to those who lead projects informally, have indirect influence on others, or even to those who work mainly on an individual basis.

There are eleven competencies divided into three clusters that make up the LGP (see Exhibit 9.1). These are the competencies deemed necessary for every leader at ULI to have in order to deliver growth and win in the marketplace, and the focus is to identify any gaps in proficiency levels for the purpose of bridging them and strengthening the competencies in question. There are four levels for each competency: foundation, developing, growth, and world class.

Exhibit 9.1 ULI's Eleven LGP Competencies

Creating a Growth Vision

1. Passion for Growth
2. Breakthrough Thinking
3. Organizational Awareness

Drives for Growth

4. Seizing the Future
5. Change Catalyst
6. Developing Self and Others
7. Holding People Accountable
8. Empowering Others

Build Commitment for Growth

9. Strategic Influencing
10. Team Commitment
11. Team Leadership

The same focus of identifying and bridging gaps applies to the development of the functional skills that need to be updated to keep up with the changes in the way work is carried out in the organization, the increasing competition, and increasing demands of consumers and customers. Recent instances when functional skills required updating was when Brand Marketing was split into Brand Development (at the regional level) and Brand Building, or when Trade Marketing was split into Trade Category Management and Customer Marketing. There was a need to delineate the roles and skill sets for each of the pair of functions as a result.

At times, certain unique capabilities also need to be obtained when the organization enters into a joint venture or acquires a new business. For example, when ULI acquired a soybean sauce company in 2000, much about soybean sauce technology had to be quickly learned, and a model for sourcing commodities such as soybean had to be developed, since the product was a novelty.

Performance Development Plan

The PDP at Unilever is not unlike any other conventional approach to performance appraisal. It is a process in which discussions on target setting, developmental plans, and career aspirations take place between superiors and their subordinates. Competency and skill gaps are identified—that is, the employee's strengths and weaknesses are fleshed out—and a clear developmental plan is mapped out that the employee is committed to follow through on and that the boss is committed to oversee and provide coaching and guidance as necessary. However, during the time when the PDP was being designed and developed, the top management team and select high-potential executives were also assigned executive coaches, in addition to their immediate bosses, to work with them on their PDPs. Under normal circumstances, however, the boss is the one who is solely responsible for his team development. HR acts only as facilitator, adviser, and policymaker. (See Exhibit 9.2 for PDP form and guidelines.)

Exhibit 9.2 Unilever Performance Development Plan and Guidelines

Performance Development Plan	(Year)
Company, Business Group or Corporate Group	_____
Name of Manager	_____
Job Title of Manager	_____
Name of Assessor	_____

This form, The Performance Development Plan, is part of the Performance Development Planning Process.

The Plan is made jointly by the manager and his/her assessor. Responsibility for achieving it is also joint. Self-development and self-assessment play an important role.

The Plan records the targets and plans as they are set the beginning of the year and completes the process at the end of the year with an assessment of how far they have been achieved. It also summarizes overall performance and views on career planning.

Exhibit 9.2 (*Continued*)

Target Setting and Review

Target	Degree Achieved		
<u>Business Results Target(s)</u> (maximum of 2)			
<u>Personal Targets</u>			

<table>
<tr><td><u>Target Set</u></td><td><u>Target Achievement</u></td></tr>
<tr><td>Manager _____</td><td>Manager _____</td></tr>
<tr><td>Assessor _____</td><td>Assessor _____</td></tr>
<tr><td>Date _____</td><td>Date _____</td></tr>
</table>

(*Continued*)

Exhibit 9.2 *(Continued)*

Skills and Competencies Development Plan

Area for Development	Improvement and Action Plan	Progress

Plan Agreed   *Progress Agreed*

Manager _____   Manager _____

Assessor _____   Assessor _____

Date _____   Date _____

Exhibit 9.2 (*Continued*)

Overall Assessment and Career Planning

Summary of Performance
Career Planning—Own Wishes
Career Planning—Company View (including potential)*

Manager _____   Signature _____   Date _____

Assessor _____   Signature _____   Date _____

Assessor's
  Superior _____   Signature _____   Date _____

*To be filled by the top management team

PDP GUIDELINES

The prime objective of PDP is to help individual managers across the business to continuously improve their own performance and that of their subordinates.

PDP process steps are as follows:

1. Review achievement of current year targets
2. Discuss next year targets
3. Review progress skills development
4. Agree skills development plan
5. Review progress competencies development
6. Agree competencies development plan
7. Record summary of performance
8. Discuss, record "own wishes"
9. Discuss, record "career plan-company view"

Abiding by the 80/20 rule, priority is placed only on two or three of the competencies or skills that are deemed most likely to make the greatest significant contributions to the business if improved. While prioritized competencies may vary for each individual, there are desired combinations of proficiency levels of competencies according to the work level (WL) of the individual. For example, for those at WL2 (manager level), most competencies must be at the developing level, with at least one competency in each cluster at growth level.

After the two or three competencies are identified as a priority for action and gap-bridging, a developmental plan is mapped out based on these prioritized competencies and the relevant training needed to bridge the gaps. However, the developmental plan does not stop here. The organization recognizes that once the individual is skilled up in the relevant target areas, the company now has a more competent employee on their hands, and they do all in their power to ensure that his or her new skills are properly channeled and utilized. This is done by exploring and charting out the range of possibilities in projects, postings, and assignments that the individual is suited to take on after she has been adequately trained. At the end of the day, the performance of individuals is linked to a variable pay component (bonus) with a sharp differentiation of rewards based on their performance. The PDP is therefore not taken lightly at ULI.

In addition, every effort is made at ULI to ensure that the notion of accountability for one's own personal development is strongly inculcated in the organizational mindset. During PDP workshops and "annual refresher workshops," employees are "drilled" on the concept of "It's my PDP," which means "I am responsible for my own career." "It's my PDP" sends home the message that the organization is unable to help you if you do not first help yourself. The employee thus feels that it is his or her responsibility to source out appropriate training programs, map out possible career paths, communicate career aspirations and training needs to his or her superior, and seize suitable career opportunities as they arise. It encourages every ULI employee to use her own prerogative to take control of her career, and to recognize that career planning is a joint partnership between employee and organization rather than an organizationally driven intervention. Perhaps the best part about "It's my PDP" is the unintended/secondary benefit it adds, in that it also inevitably fosters an overall culture of accountability where work and office relationships are concerned. This is because if every individual felt some sense of responsibility for his own career, then that feeling would naturally extend to all aspects of career planning, including how work duties are carried out and how colleagues (whether superiors, peers, or subordinates) are treated in the course of it.

Balanced Business Plan

ULI has an initiative called "Strategy Into Action," which is a process for mobilizing the whole organization to achieve strategic intent. It is a cycle of think, plan, deliver, and review. The output is a Balanced Business Plan document for corporate ULI and for each division that clearly states goals, priorities, measures, and targets for the entire organization and each division in turn. This is presented on a kind of one-page balanced scorecard in terms of market, operation, people and organization, and financial outcome (see Exhibit 9.3).

The goals and hence priorities of the company and divisions are then translated into departmental goals using the same BBP format, and whenever relevant, into individual goals and targets on the employees' PDPs.

HR Planning Sessions

Core to succession planning at ULI are the HR planning sessions that are conducted jointly with every division throughout the organization. The scope of these meetings cover:

- Talent review
  - —List of high potentials (HPs) and sustained high performers (SHPs)

Exhibit 9.3 ULI's Balanced Business Plan Form for 2006

Unilever Indonesia
Corporate Balanced Business Plan   2006

Unilever mission	*Vitality mission*	*ULI values*
• Be the first and best in class in meeting the needs and aspirations of consumers • Be the most preferred partner to our customers, suppliers and community • Remove non value-added activities from all processes • Employer of choice for high-performance people • Aim for stretching targets for profitable growth and secure above-average rewards for employees and shareholders • Earn respect for integrity, care for community and environment	Our mission is to add vitality to life. We meet everyday needs for nutrition, hygiene, and personal care with brands that help people feel good, look good and get more out of life.	• Customer, consumer and community focus • Teamwork • Integrity • Making things happen • Sharing of joy • Excellence

Marketplace	*Operations*	*People and Organization*	*Financial Outcomes*
• Goals and measurements	• Goals and measurements	• Goals and measurements	• Goals and measurements

We will achieve these goals through these key strategic initiatives . . .

—List of low performers who need serious attention

—Local outpostings/expatriation

- Forced ranking

  —Performance versus potential

- Succession pipeline
- New appointments
- Organization structure

  —Current versus future

HR planning sessions are carried out on an annual basis, first at divisional level, then at corporate level. The management development manager and HR director arrange for individual meetings with the respective divisional directors first, before meeting with the top management team together. Depending on the number of people covered and the complexity of issues for the division, several meetings may need to take place with the same division before the final top management team meeting. This crucial planning process ranks high on the top management team's and directors' priority lists, and because of this, the level of efficiency with which the meetings are carried out normally drives the entire planning process to completion within two weeks.

Forced Ranking

Rightly or wrongly, the forced ranking process is normally the one that carries the weight of the succession planning system on its shoulders. Much of the talent review and succession pipeline depends on the forced ranking system and how it is implemented. The impact and effects of forced ranking are far-reaching for succession planning and often warrant close attention. Similar to General Electric's nine-block rating system of potential versus performance for its employees, Unilever too has a nine-box matrix in which every individual is placed. One axis indicates the potential of

Exhibit 9.4　Unilever's Forced Ranking Matrix

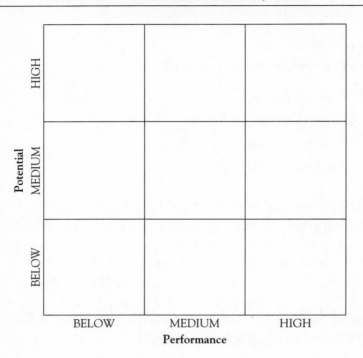

the employee, while the other indicates the performance, both areas ranked high, medium, and below (see Exhibit 9.4). *Performance* is about how skills and competencies are applied to deliver results, and *potential* is about personal aptitude to reach higher work levels.

Where the individual is placed in the matrix depends upon the assessment made by the concerned director, with inputs from the individual's superior on his performance and potential, usually based on the individual's PDP report. This is done first by the division, and then at corporate level with all the top management team members. Candidates with high potential to reach WL3 (level reporting to the top management team) would need top management team approval, whereas those with potential to reach a level lower than WL3 can be decided upon by directors and HR.

The results of the matrix then form the basis of the high potential (HP) and sustained high performer (SHP) lists. Put simply, HPs are those who have high potential and deliver good results, and SHPs are those who continuously deliver good results but may not have the potential to progress beyond their current work levels. First priority will be given to those on the HP lists for any vacancy at any level that requires promotion from within, and they will also be considered for any expatriate opportunities that arise.

Top Succession

Preparing for top succession at ULI is a rigorous process involving active participation and decision making from the top management team. The hands-on involvement of the top management team in top succession planning is a nonnegotiable and is seen to be one of the major contributing factors to the success of the program. The process is described as a "discipline" that takes place every year to discuss and debate over who needs to be prepared for top management team succession or next level succession. HR is certainly not the sole owner of this process. In fact, top succession is seen as the responsibility of the entire top team.

If a name is put up for recommendation and there are no top management team supporters, this automatically disqualifies the candidate from further consideration. The rules are stringent and demand that a minimum of three top management team members other than the candidate's own sponsor show support and give endorsement for the candidate to take on the next key position or level. That is, without ample buy-in and sponsorship of the top management team, top succession planning would not be possible.

Once it is decided who is top management team material, the next question is, Where does she fit? Take note that while it is decided that an incumbent is top management team material, plans for her next move may not necessarily be vertical. The important factor to take into account is not only what the best job fit is in order for her to realize her potential, but also what move could give her the greatest exposure and make her the most well rounded. And once those questions are answered, immediate preparation is made for the incumbent to move into her new position seamlessly. This is normally accomplished through a well-planned handover period. An efficient and customized "on-boarding" process in top succession is another major contributor to ULI's success in succession planning, and takes place on two levels:

1. *On a personal performance assessment level.* The individual is prepared in advance for the new job and subsequently coached in the crucial first 100 days on what needs to be done and how to do it.

2. *On a structural and organizational level.* The nature of jobs (that is, job descriptions) is always changed and reshaped if necessary to fit the talents and strengths of the incumbents rather than the other way around (that is, slotting incumbents into fixed pigeonholes). In addition, parts of the job that are not well suited for the incumbent or are not an area of strength for him are carved out and assigned to someone better able to perform the function. The mistake that many organizations make in succession planning is in treating it as a box-filling exercise. At ULI, top jobs are often reshaped and restructured to ensure each individual's success in the job as he or she move up in the organization.

Talent Development

Last but not least, there are a range of supplementary talent development initiatives, both formal and informal, that are part of the succession planning mechanism and that employees benefit from. From coaching and mentoring and career counseling to other leadership development initiatives, ULI shores up and sustains the main succession planning mechanisms by supporting them with efforts that encourage continuous development and improvement of leaders, teams, and individuals. For example, while the clarity of a good development plan helps to motivate future potential leaders in the organization, regular coaching (whether by an internal or external coach) helps increase the commitment on the part of the individual to follow through with his developmental plan, while mentoring helps to manage his expectations.

There are several ways in which coaching takes place at ULI:

1. *External consultants* are hired to become the executive coaches of a selected few in the top echelons of the organization.

2. *Managers* are skilled up with the necessary coaching competencies and exposed to coaching tools and techniques, as in the Senior Executive Development Program (SEDP; see section later in chapter on "Key Leadership Development Initiatives").

3. The concept of informal *peer coaching* was recently introduced via the MCR buddy program.

4. *Generative coaching* is provided by those in WL4 or WL3 for their subordinates (see section on "The Generative Coaching Model").

Instilling a coaching culture and mindset at ULI is seen to promote openness and trust among team members, which in turn helps to retain top talents. In fact, a coaching culture was regarded as such a valuable asset to the organization that ULI hired a consultant to help them build it. While most companies may talk about the benefits of having a coaching culture, ULI meant serious business and took the necessary steps to put the building blocks of their desired culture in place. They not only wanted a coaching culture, but one that could create excitement and passion in its people. First, the top management team set an example for the entire organization in supporting and building a coaching culture, which began with the chairman taking on executive coaching, followed by the rest of the top team. This sent the message that nobody was too high up in the organization, or too successful in their careers, to be beyond executive coaching. In fact, both the previous and current chairmen of ULI desired and received executive coaching. Thus the culture of coaching and being willing to be coached was set right from the top of the organization and easily filtered its way down to the rest.

Key Leadership Development Initiatives. ULI launched their key leadership development initiatives by engaging external consultants to carry out executive coaching for the chairman and selected members of the top management team. This was followed by the roll-out of a Senior Executive Development Program to the top 100 in the organization. The SEDP consisted of three-day leadership development workshops facilitated by external consultants, which helped executives align their source of energy (that is, what they *want* to do), execution abilities (that is, what they *can* do), and organizational or personal expectations of themselves (that is, what they *should* do). (See Figure 9.2.)

The SEDP helped executives appreciate and see facets of themselves and their leadership styles and abilities (and those of others) where they previously could not, so that they were able to channel their motivations, competencies, and values to obtain optimum output and results for organizational as well as personal benefit. Day 1 of the workshop explored the learning tactics, personality types, and motivations of the executives through a variety of assessment tools

Figure 9.2 ULI's Want-Can-Should Model for Senior Executive Development Program

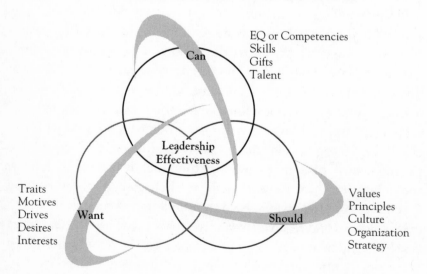

© Linkage_Asia Pte. Ltd.

and lecturettes. Day 2 covered the use of competencies, personal proficiency levels of competencies, and executive derailment through the use of 360-degree feedback reports, lecturettes, and action learning. Day 3 focused on dealing with the real job challenges in the workplace and taking steps to develop a personal action plan.

In addition to the three-day SEDP, one-day coaching workshops were conducted for the same group of senior executives at ULI to equip them with the necessary coaching competencies and expose them to several coaching tools, techniques, and models; for example, the GAPS (Goals-Abilities-Perceptions-Standards) model, and the GROW (Goal-Reality-Options-Wrap-up) and Skill-Will models by Max Landsberg.

The Generative Coaching Model.   As part of building a coaching culture within the organization, ULI adopted a Generative Coaching Model (GCM), which its managers and those in leadership positions could utilize for the facilitation of coaching and team relationships. ULI had engaged consultants Erehwon to help them build their coaching culture. The model includes tools such as Delayering, Open House, and Interpersonal Alignment, which encourage High Openness, High Alignment, and High Initiative (see Exhibit 9.5).

The philosophy behind GCM is that in any discussion, openness in that discussion is superficial until you touch a personal level involving values. Even when a heated discussion or debate ensues, it is still only taking place at a professional level unless values are brought in. While a discussion may seem open and candid, it is not truly open until a personal level is reached. This model has caused positive ripples throughout the organization that are reflected by the new level of openness of people during meetings and their willingness to talk about the "brutal facts." It is also hoped that this model will become a very powerful tool in succession planning. That is, if the basis and assumption of the model is not to make any assumptions, then the organization can learn to dig deeper and "delayer" its employees to find out their true career aspirations and hopes so that ULI is better equipped to prepare them for their journey ahead in the company.

Exhibit 9.5 Building A Generative Coaching Culture

The current context at Unilever Indonesia

Unilever Indonesia's desire is to be not just a good company, but a great company. Hence the organization's long-term vision and need is to create a large and vibrant pool of future growth leaders. This can only happen when the current leaders in the organization go beyond being a driver of business results to becoming a generative coach: *focusing on building future growth leaders*.

Generative Leadership

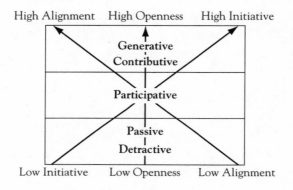

The Leader as Generative Coach: The 4-Level Process

| Level 4 | Increasing number of future leaders |

A Level 4 leader is able to institutionalize practices to cultivate future leaders, consistently. He is able to create great creative challenges, and enable people to deliver on those challenges.

| Level 3 | Increasing number of performance initiatives |

A Level 3 leader is consciously able to build performance enabling practices, focusing not only on enabling individual performance but also team performance.

| Level 2 | Increasing ownership and commitment |

A Level 2 leader is able to build high levels of ownership and commitment.

| Level 1 | Increasing openness and transparency |

A Level 1 leader is able to create an environment that promotes a high level of openness and transparency.

Source: Erehwon Innovative Consulting

Feedback and Analysis

While yearly reviews are carried out on the succession planning system at ULI, changes made to the system are usually not major, as the basic principles around which the system is centered are soundly anchored. For example, new talent pools may arise as a result of emerging business needs, or the way that competencies are evaluated may need to be updated using a new competency model, but the basic principles such as corporate and functional talent pools and forced ranking are always maintained.

Other ways in which the succession planning system is reinforced throughout the organization are the use of one-day PDP refresher workshops at which managers can be refreshed on PDP concepts. The workshops are usually conducted annually, spread over a period of two weeks so that those interested can take part in the workshop on any day convenient to them.

Evaluation

While there are no predetermined criteria, key performance indicators, or outputs by which ULI measures the effectiveness of their succession planning system, the instruments are always present and the results accessible. There are two basic types of evaluation that ULI is able to tap into: internal and external evaluations.

Internal Evaluations

Global People Survey. The Global People Survey is conducted every two years, and the objective is to learn more about how Unilever people see their organization based on a set of twelve attributes (see Exhibit 9.6). The survey helps Unilever to listen to, involve, and energize its people, and to support its leaders in creating real change.

The results of the survey on the Valuing People attribute acts as an indicator to show how well ULI is performing in the eyes of its people where succession planning is concerned. And past data has shown that ULI usually fares better on this attribute than other

---

Exhibit 9.6 Unilever's Global People Survey Groups of Attributes

1. Leadership
2. Valuing people
3. Strategic focus
4. My department
5. Immediate boss
6. My job
7. Commitment
8. Personal development
9. Reward
10. Customer orientation
11. Managing change
12. Organization responsibility

Unilever companies, as its people feel that ULI does a good job in promoting the most competent people.

Interim Pulse Check. The Pulse Check is an interim survey to assess whether any follow-up action plans were successfully implemented as a result of the Global People Survey.

Employee Trends. The retention levels of staff and recruitment success rates at ULI are perhaps the most encouraging signs and measures of success that speak for the effectiveness of its succession planning system. On an annual basis, the organization maintains an approximate 98-percent retention level of its employees across the board, and a 75–80-percent recruitment success rate.

In addition, there are an increasing number of Indonesian managers taking on regional roles or overseas postings. Currently, as many as 10 percent of these managers hold regional portfolios or are working overseas.

Global Ranking. Within the Unilever world, ULI remains one of the best-performing companies in terms of operating profits and revenue, and is also recognized as one of the best in building an enterprise culture.

Audit Systems. Audit systems are available for selected programs, such as the generative coaching program. Erehwon is now in the process of conducting an audit to assess the implementation of the generative coaching program in ULI and to identify future improvements. The audit is done using one-to-one interviews with the leaders of the organization (in this case, WL3 executives) and focus group discussions with the teams reporting to these leaders. Some of the issues discussed are the level of openness in the organization, and whether work relationships and performance has seen improvements as a result of the program.

External Evaluations

The icing on the cake for ULI in terms of assessing how well it is doing with its people strategy is decidedly the numerous awards it receives from renowned business magazines and publications, for example, the Best Employer Award for Indonesia from the *Warta Ekonomi* magazine in 2004 (see Exhibit 9.7). While awards like the Best Employer Award do not specifically point to the effectiveness of the organization's succession planning system per se, receiving such awards reflects on how the organization treats people, whether it provides employees with clear career paths and opportunities for wider challenges, growth and advancement, and develops their knowledge and capabilities adequately.

Overall Evaluations: Beyond Hard Measures

If one were to look critically at the holistic succession planning system in place at ULI, and ask whether it has accomplished what it was set up to accomplish, many in the organization would without doubt answer in the affirmative. Even without the hard measures or the many awards, the leaders at ULI can say honestly and proudly that they have been able to maintain a continuous flow of good

Exhibit 9.7 ULI Awards Received During 2005

No.	Awards	From	Date	Remarks
1.	Best Employer Award 2004	• Warta Ekonomi Magazine	December 2005	Ranked No. 1
2.	Zero Accident Award 2004	• Dept of Manpower & Transmigration	Trophy given on 17 January 2005	
3.	The Indonesian Customer Loyalty Award 2005	• SWA and MARS	24 January 2005	• Lux (toiletries-bar soap) • Vaseline (cosmetics) • Pond's (cosmetics)
4.	The Most Effective Ads in 2004	• Marketing Research Indonesia	26 January 2005	Pepsodent family TV ad (Lowe)
5.	Call Center Award 2005	• Marketing Magazine and Center for Customer Satisfaction and Loyalty	9 March 2005	Consumer advisory
6.	Good Corporate Governance	• The Asset magazine	March 2005	Number one in Indonesia
7.	Adoi Advertising Awards 2004	• LOWE	Award given on April 2005	Unilever Indonesia is Client of the Year
8.	Rekor Indonesia 2005	• MURI	18 June 2005	Unilever Indonesia (Clear Gel), as pioneer and 90° Fashion Show organizer in Indonesia
9.	Top 10 Favorite CEOs 2005	• Survey by Warta Ekonomi magazine	13 June 2005	ULI Chairman, Maurits Lalisang elected as 1 of the 10 favorite CEOs 2005. (Rank 7)
10.	Golden Indonesian Best Brand Award (IBBA) 2005	SWA Magazine and MARS	29 June 2005	• Sunlight (liquid dish soap) • Sunsilk (shampoo) • Lifebuoy (bar soap) • Lux (liquid soap) • Pepsodent (toothpaste) • Citra (hand and body lotion) • Pond's (face whitening) • Rinso (powder detergent) • Molto (fabric softener)
11.	Indonesian Most Admired Knowledge Enterprise (MAKE) 2005	• Dunamis Organisation Services, Indonesia	21 July 2005	Number one in Indonesia

Exhibit 9.7 (*Continued*)

No.	Awards	From	Date	Remarks
12.	Asia's Best Companies 2005	• *FinanceAsia*	July 2005	• Most committed to strong dividend policy–Rank 2 • Best corporate governance–Rank 6 • Best managed company–Rank 7
13.	Indonesia's Most Admired Companies (IMAC 2005)	• *Business Week* Magazine and Frontier (Research Agency)	August 2005	• Toiletries category
14.	Indonesian Customer Satisfaction Award (ICSA) 2005	*SWA Sembada* Magazine and Frontier (Research Agency)	30 Sep 2005	• Sariwangi (tea bag) • Blue Band (margarine) • Lifebuoy (bar shop) • Sunsilk (shampoo) • Citra (hand and body lotion) • Rexona (deodorant) • Pepsodent (toothpaste) • Rinso (powder detergent) • Molto (fabric softener)
15.	Asian Most Admired Knowledge Enterprise (MAKE) Award 2005	Teleos, UK	14 Oct 2005	For the following criteria: • Creating an environment for collaborative knowledge sharing • Creating a learning organization
16.	Value Champs–The top 50 Management Teams in Asia	*CFO Asia* Magazine	14 Oct 2005	Ranked 39 among top 50 management teams in Asia • Among the few highest in 5-year annual average total shareholder return
17.	Economic Value Added (EVA) Award 2005	*SWA Sembada* Magazine and Frontier (Research Agency)	23 Oct 2005	Golden EVA 2005 (3 years EVA)
18.	International Energy Globe Award 2005	Energy Globe, Austria	19 Nov 2005	Environment 1st prize for water category
19.	e-Banking Indonesia Award 2005	Citigroup Indonesia	30 Nov 2005	"Early adopter of e-banking" category

(Continued)

Exhibit 9.7 (*Continued*)

No.	Awards	From	Date	Remarks
20.	**Packaging Consumer Branding Awards 2005**	*SWA magazine* and *Mix Marketing* magazine	5 Dec 2005	**Rank 1** • Wall's (ice cream) • Kecap Bango (soy sauce) • Blue Band (margarine) • SariWangi (teabags) • Rinso (detergents) • Molto (fabric softener) • Sunlight (liquid dishwash) • Sunlight (cream dishwash) • Superpell (liquid floor cleaner) • Lux (cosmetic bar soap) • Lifebuoy (bar soap) • Pepsodent (toothpaste) • Sunsilk (shampoo) **Rank 2** • Taro (snack) • Domestos Nomos (insecticide incense) • Dove (cosmetic bar soap) • Close Up (toothpaste) • Pepsodent (toothbrush) • Clear (shampoo) **Rank 3** • Pepsodent (mouthwash) • Huggies (baby diapers) • Domestos Wipol (liquid floor cleaner) **Rank 4** • Surf (detergent) • Kotex (pantyliners) **Rank 5** • Lifebuoy (shampoo)

managers and key talent in the system for promotions, postings, appointments, and, of course, succession. Though it is a "soft" measure, having the succession pipeline continuously filled with bright and promising talent can be considered to be one of the most critical and telling measures of a company's success. What is a succession planning system without the main tool (that is, the pipeline) for its implementation? Without achieving this critical success factor, it would have been impossible for ULI to attain the positive results that it had for the other hard measures.

Working diversity and flexibility into its talent pools has also created breakthroughs in learning at ULI as new and different perspectives are mixed with old and established ideas; and also because employees are better prepared for and even encouraged to take on cross-functional or regional roles. ULI has proven its ability to accommodate big changes in the organization structure and is able to say with some measure of confidence that it has the flexibility to move their available talented resources across functions.

A real company success story that demonstrates this flexibility was when one of their HR managers effectively took on the role of marketing manager. When the organization underwent business process reengineering to cut unnecessary processes in the company, the HR manager was made responsible for overseeing this initiative and finding the solution. From HR manager, he then became corporate planner and took on one or two more roles to expand his portfolio. At the time, the HR manager decided that since he had already taken on a few roles, it would do no harm to try out marketing as well. As it turned out, that was where he discovered a real interest and was able to harness his talents and skills most effectively. Today, the once-HR manager is excelling in his new role as marketing manager.

Lessons Learned

Lesson 1: *Don't make assumptions about your people.*

When making long-term plans for your talent, don't make the mistake of assuming that the best career path for her in the organization is the one she is currently on, or the one that matches her academic qualifications. Make effort to find out if she has other interests and strengths through stretch assignments, job rotation, or added new responsibilities that you can optimize to serve the organization better. This also builds greater flexibility into your talent pool and, as a result, your succession planning system.

Lesson 2: *Build diversity into your talent pool.*

Any best-practice organization will recognize that diversity is critical. With globalization and regionalization at the forefront, having a diverse workforce is now essential for understanding and operating in the global marketplace effectively. Mixing new and different perspectives with old and established ideas also fosters a learning environment and keeps the organization from stagnating and becoming obsolete in the fast-changing world we live in. The talent pool will therefore need continual rejuvenation to ensure that there is no shortage of diverse talents coming down the pipeline.

Lesson 3: *Prepare the incumbent for the next big job.*

Many executives make the assumption that somebody performing well at one level means he will also be able to perform well at the next level. This may be true for certain cases, but ill preparation of the incumbent when promoting him to a level that involves managing a team when previously there was none, or managing a cross-functional team as opposed to a singular one, is a setup for failure. Preparation here could include helping him build networks, skill development in people or team management, training in the appropriate functional skills, or simply just having more cross-functional projects throughout the organization.

Interestingly, experience has shown that an individual could be a tremendous leader when running a factory with hundreds of subordinates, but when tasked to lead a cross-functional project with just ten people, he flounders because there had been no preparation.

Lesson 4: *Custom-fit key jobs for top individuals.*

Remember that succession planning is not a box-filling exercise. Instead, key jobs should be reshaped and restructured to fit the talents and strengths of incumbents in order for them to excel in their new jobs. This not only ensures the most optimal output from incumbents, to achieve the best results, but also heightens employee commitment and job satisfaction.

Lesson 5: *Get involvement and buy-in at all levels.*

A succession planning system cannot be effective without the involvement and buy-in of the entire organization. In fact, the relationship between cause and effect is directly proportional: the greater the involvement and buy-in, the more effective the system becomes. This is because making the system work relies on the commitment and ownership of all the stakeholders. Sponsorship from the top level is crucial to drive the entire process (especially that of top succession planning), and top leaders need to cascade their commitment and beliefs in the system by demonstrating support and flexibility to whatever will make the system work best. HR and managers need to maintain discipline and focus in selecting, identifying, and developing talent to build a dynamic and diverse talent pool. And all employees need to take responsibility for their own career and continually improve and develop themselves for their own benefit as well as that of the organization.

In order to achieve this, there must first be a culture that supports the basic principles and philosophy behind the succession planning system, together with the policies and procedures that gain maximum involvement from all stakeholders. Last but not least, an effective communication plan that educates and instills these practices is the channel through which the buy-in and involvement are obtained.

Lesson 6: *Create a coaching culture.*

Creating a coaching culture will greatly enhance and complement your succession planning system. It not only creates an environment that encourages continuous learning and elicits greater commitment to follow-up on developmental action plans, but it can also build openness and trust in boss-subordinate and peer relationships if done properly. Having a coaching culture will also open the lines of communication and feedback on how to better align personal and organizational goals and interests.

About the Contributors

Josef Bataona is human resource director and a board member of PT Unilever Indonesia. He has been in the HR field for more than twenty-five years, in local as well as regional roles covering operations in several countries in the Asian region. With Unilever Indonesia's business turnover of US$1 billion, Josef is currently responsible for 3,000 employees. His experience covers a wide gamut of HR practices, and he is seen both as HR business partner as well as HR expert within the global Unilever setup, as well as on a country-specific basis. Having this broad spectrum of HR responsibilities is seen as a necessity in order to compete in the marketplace. The rich and varied HR portfolio that Josef possesses has made him an experienced HR practitioner, and has helped Unilever Indonesia to be acknowledged and recognized as a best-practice and benchmark company in the Indonesian HR market. This reputation and other achievements in HR excellence were gained based on Josef's belief that "we can only grow the business if we grow people." His own personal motto is: "Be yourself, but better every day."

Desley Khew served as consultant and facilitator in Unilever Indonesia's Senior Executive Development Program and was involved in the design and development of the program. She is currently a consultant with Linkage_Asia.

Samuel M. Lam is president of Linkage_Asia and served as executive coach to both the current and previous chairmen of Unilever Indonesia, as well as other members of the top management team. Sam was the lead consultant for Unilever Indonesia's leadership development initiatives, including the SEDP. He also serves as executive coach and adviser to a number of notable chief executive officers and senior government officials in Singapore, Asia, and Europe. His expertise is in the area of leadership development, executive coaching, executive selection, performance improvement of top teams and talent management. Sam designs and delivers leadership development programs for both public sector and global multinational firms.

Part Three

SUCCESSION PLANNING TOOLKIT

10

INTRODUCTION TO THE TOOLKIT

David Giber

As shown in Figure 10.1, the entire succession process can be accurately divided into eight major "phases." These phases, organized chronologically for the sake of simplicity, may not always occur in the exact order. All of these must be considered, understood, and addressed to implement a successful succession initiative.

Part Three of *Best Practices for Succession Planning* is dedicated to the explanation and portrayal of these essential phases of succession. This chapter provides a brief description of the three phases and how they affect the overall process.

In addition to this, there are a number of tools that are used to define each of succession and provide a hands-on learning approach. These tools and assessments are organized and discussed in detail in the rest of the chapters in Part Three.

The succession management cycle in Figure 10.1 may seem detailed, but it is meant for the practitioner, not the client. Through it, we at Linkage have created a blueprint for the phases one needs to take to ensure effectiveness at every stage of the cycle. The first phase is *developing the business case* for succession in terms of cost and benefits and organizational readiness. If this is done thoroughly, many of the considerations for the next phases of *creating the architecture* and *designing and planning the implementation* of the system will emerge from a comprehensive assessment. In Chapter Eleven, we provide examples of tools that help drive these early phases and build a strong foundation to the succession work.

The heart of any succession project is *development*; this includes *analyzing bench strength*, *identifying specific successors* and reviewing

Figure 10.1 Best-Practice Succession Management Cycle

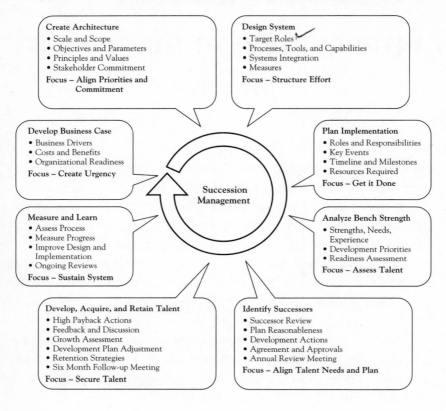

their strengths and development needs, and putting together over-all plans for the phase *developing, acquiring, and retaining talent for the future*. We include in Chapter Twelve a set of tools on this critical area as well. The quality of development planning, the thorough-ness of the feedback, mentoring, coaching, or on-the-job training provided is where participants will judge how serious the company is about the succession effort.

Finally, there is the measure and learn, or *evaluation phase*, which includes the key step of measuring and learning about how well the system is performing based on metrics connected to the human resource (HR) management system and the business itself, the effectiveness of the individual development follow-through, and the growth of capabilities among key players in the organization. The tools presented in Chapter Thirteen are focused on launching, sustaining, and measuring an effective overall succession system. It is designed to introduce you to a set of tools to "jump-start" your ability to move your organization through these critical phases and steps in the succession management cycle. This means assessing the readiness of the organization to accept and utilize the succession systems as well as having the right measures for whether the system is impacting the business and addressing the areas where talent can drive business competitiveness and success.

Objectives
scale
Principles +values

11

ASSESSMENT TOOLS

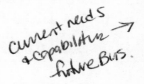

current needs
+ capabilities →
future Bus.

The first critical phase in the succession planning cycle is assessment. *Assessment*, in terms of succession planning, means several things. Obviously, it entails assessing the candidates themselves. There are a variety of strategic choices that can be made as to how that assessment is structured, what instruments or processes are used, and how the information is shared with the candidate. Assessment must be based on a review of the capabilities needed to drive the organization toward the future, determining the balance of personal, business, and other characteristics that need to be assessed. If the succession process is positioned as one that provides development feedback and acts as a catalyst to development for the candidates and their managers, then the assessment process must mirror that development emphasis. This means offering a range of assessments that raise questions for the candidates about where they need to develop and prompt them to examine both their strengths as leaders and managers and their development gaps.

Succession assessment also means assessing the talent needs of the organization. Many organizations do not assess their talent needs (and current strengths) against their future strategies. What is most useful is even to go beyond this and ask, "What talent and capabilities could we build or acquire that could create a competitive advantage that we do not currently have?" Few firms use talent and succession planning as a proactive weapon to think about how it could help them leapfrog the competition into a new area and change the limits on a business paradigm. Organizations may also make the mistake of positioning succession management as an HR program rather than a senior management imperative. An assessment can help reposition your succession initiative and assure that the scope of your project is clear, practical, and will have impact.

This chapter describes four assessment tools. The first tool, called the Stages of Succession Process Checklist and presented in Exhibit 11.1, is used in the early stages of a succession process. It is

Exhibit 11.1 The Stages of Succession Process Checklist

What It Is:
- This tool contains a chart to help you identify the key people responsible for developing, designing, and implementing a succession plan. The tool specifically targets the roles and responsibilities that must be assigned and undertaken in order for the process to be successful.

When to Use It:
- It can be best used at the early planning stages of a succession process, but it will be important to revisit at each phase as the initiative moves forward.

How to Use It:
- This tool should be the backdrop for a discussion about roles and responsibilities in the implementation team. Once the team has sorted out who is doing what, it can be used to identify key stakeholders, sponsors, and subject matter experts who may need to be involved with the process, what degree of support is necessary, and what actions should be taken.

Developing the Business Case

Stage		People Responsible	Degree of Support (High, Medium, Low)	Actions
Purpose	To identify relevant context, parameters, and needs for succession			
Key Activities	• Capture critical elements of future direction of organization for succession • Identify external factors impacting succession • Analyze organizational systems and culture impacting succession • Forecast the types and quantities of leadership talent needed • Define key strategic drivers and scope for succession system			
Useful Integration Points	• Strategic planning process • HR planning process			

Exhibit 11.1 (*Continued*)

Key Roles and Responsibilities		Who?	Degree of Support (High, Medium, Low)	Actions
Champion	Work with senior HR leader to identify key strategic drivers and talent needs			
Senior HR Leader	Work with EDO to form succession structure to support strategic drivers and talent requirements to maximize value add to business			
Executive Development Office (EDO)	Define the preliminary succession scope, architecture, and implementation timeline for review with senior management			
EDO & HR Business Partner	Meet with key line people and identify: – Business drivers – Talent needs – Customer requirements – Gaps, risks, issues, and opportunities			
Senior Management Team & Line Management (level depends on reach of MS Process)	• Communicate business requirements for MSP design • Identify current and future talent needs • Provide a preliminary set of program needs for design consideration –Scope –Key jobs –Sense of current talent bench –Gaps to be addressed (in bench, diversity, etc.) –Risks and issues (i.e., workload, readiness of replacements, etc.) –Opportunities (deep/ broad bench, local development opportunities, mentors, etc.)			

(*Continued*)

Exhibit 11.1 *(Continued)*

Creating the Architecture

Stage		People Responsible	Degree of Support (High, Medium, Low)	Actions
Purpose	To create a systematic approach to addressing succession needs			
Key Activities	• Determine scale and scope of effort • Define objectives • Identify guiding principles and values • Solidify stakeholder commitment			
Useful Integration Points	• Performance management system • Career development system • Staffing and promotion systems • Reward and recognition systems			

Key Roles and Responsibilities		Who?	Degree of Support	Actions
Champion	Work with senior HR leader and EDO to review mission, vision, goals and guiding principles, targeted roles, and preliminary design for succession system			
Senior HR Leader	Work with EDO to develop objectives and guiding principles, targeted roles, and preliminary design for succession system			
Executive Development Office (EDO)	• Develop recommendations for mission, vision, goals and guiding principles, targeted roles, and preliminary design for succession system • Develop talent acquisition, retention, and strategic staffing recommendations • Develop preliminary plan for operational integration with other HR systems			

Exhibit 11.1 (*Continued*)

Key Roles and Responsibilities		Who?	Degree of Support	Actions
EDO & HR Business Partner	• Obtain input on goals and guiding principles, targeted roles, and preliminary design for succession system ➤ • Obtain input on talent needs, acquisition, and retention for strategic consideration • Discuss preliminary operational considerations for implementation • Review integration points with other HR systems			
Senior Management Team and Line Management (level depends on reach of MS Process)	• Provide input on goals and guiding principles, targeted roles, and preliminary design for succession system • Provide input on talent needs, acquisition, and retention for strategic consideration ➤ • Provide other information as required for design and preliminary implementation considerations • Review and final architectural components with champion/EDO (senior management team)			

aimed at helping the practitioner challenge his or her own thinking about whether the succession process is correctly positioned within the organization and whether the key connections to stakeholders and other human resources (HR) and organizational development processes have been made. This tool lays out the evolving nature of the key roles and responsibilities of the major stakeholders to the succession process, and provides room to note issues that may arise in terms of stakeholder commitment, integration with other HR processes, and key activities that must be completed to move to the next phase.

The Readiness Assessment (see Exhibit 11.2) is our second tool and is also valuable at the beginning of a succession process,

Exhibit 11.2 The Readiness Assessment

What It Is:

- This survey is aimed at driving a discussion to surface the organization's readiness to drive succession management and talent planning.

When to Use It:

- The survey is best used before moving into designing the succession architecture and planning how the succession process is connected to the organization's culture and tied into the larger talent and human resource management systems.

How to Use It:

- This survey is meant as a "dialogue provoker" among the senior management team and/or the stakeholders involved with succession management.

- *The critical part of the survey is not the ratings but is the rationale which the team can share about why they wrote in certain scores.* The point is to help the team identify potential areas where they may encounter roadblocks or inconsistencies with what they are trying to achieve through succession management and current company beliefs and practices.

- The tool will also help surface areas where the succession process is well supported by the company and where this alignment can be capitalized on. To use the tool, simply ask people to rate the readiness of the organization in terms of these fifteen factors from 0–100 percent.

Percentage (0–100)	Readiness Factors	Rationale for Ratings
	Business Drivers—Factors influencing the need for succession management efforts are clear, valid, and compelling.	
	Organizational Change—Experience with successful organizational change, including responsiveness to the need for change, effective change process, and achievement of objectives.	
	Measurement—Organization has clear, aligned measures for assessing performance of individuals, teams, programs, and the organization overall.	
	Leadership—Leaders are viewed as effective in providing direction for the business and leading both individuals and teams toward the achievement of key goals and strategies.	
	Morale—Employees enjoy working in the organization and believe in its mission, values, and key strategies.	

Exhibit 11.2 *(Continued)*

Percentage (0–100)	Readiness Factors	Rationale for Ratings
	Integrity and Fairness—Business and people decisions are perceived to be based on a clear sense of integrity; people believe they and others are treated fairly by their management and the organization.	
	Rewards—Recognition and reward systems align individual and organizational success.	
	Organizational Structure—Structure supports the direction and key strategies of the organization, fosters timely and effective decision making, and creates needed accountability and shared responsibility.	
	Process Orientation—Business and HR systems are supported by clear and effective processes that are used consistently in the organization (i.e., influencing receptivity to processes to support succession).	
	Communication—Essential vertical and horizontal communication vehicles exist to support information flow, learning, and decision making.	
	Leadership Challenges and Capabilities—Challenges and capabilities for key levels in the organization (e.g., individual contributor, supervisor, manager, executive) are well understood.	
	Performance Management Systems—Systems exist to support effective goal setting, ongoing monitoring, and evaluation of individual and team performance with attention to both results and capabilities for success.	
	Development Systems and Culture—Individuals and their managers invest time and energy in developing the capabilities needed for effective performance and career progression. Managers engage in providing useful feedback and coaching to support the development and performance of their people.	

(Continued)

Exhibit 11.2 (*Continued*)

Percentage (0–100)	Readiness Factors	Rationale for Ratings
	Transitions—Systems exist to support key transitions in the organization (e.g., information, development, network of support).	
	Sponsorship—The sponsor(s) of the effort are at the appropriate level, invested in succession, well respected in the organization, and have the authority to make the policy and resource decisions needed to guide the effort.	

Results of Readiness Assessment

	0	25	50	75	100
Business drivers					
Organizational change					
Measurement					
Leadership					
Morale					
Integrity and fairness					
Rewards					
Organizational structure					
Process orientation					
Communication					
Leadership challenges and capabilities					
Performance management systems					
Development systems and culture					
Transitions					
Sponsorship					

although it could also be used to drive a discussion as to whether a succession process is having the desired strategic impact. It outlines fifteen major areas that directly relate to succession and the ability to drive a successful system. Using it with a management team, the consultant can easily discern where there are current holes or likely gaps and obstacles that will need to be addressed as the succession process evolves. For a succession project to be successful, the consultant must connect various organizational systems in order to build a business rationale and logic.

A third assessment tool similar to Linkage's Readiness Assessments is William Rothwell's Checksheet for Assessing the Organization's Technical Succession Practices (Exhibit 11.3).

Exhibit 11.3 A Checksheet for Assessing the Organization's Technical Succession Planning Practices

What It Is:
- *Technical succession planning* is, quite literally, planning for the continuity of technical and professional workers whose special, unique and often proprietary knowledge of the business is essential to sustaining competitive advantage. A technical succession planning program is thus focused as much around preserving institutional memory as it is finding or developing replacements for key positions.
- This checksheet allows users to rate their organizations for how well they are planning for preserving institutional memory in the face of pending losses due to retirements, sudden departures from the organization, or other losses of technical or professional talent.

When to Use It:
- Use this checksheet as a starting point for opening a conversation about how well the managers of an organization are preparing for the loss of institutional memory—particularly among technical workers such as engineers, management information systems professionals, research scientists, or other such people with special knowledge.
- Ask the manager(s) of technical or professional departments to complete the checksheet and then feed it back for discussion to senior managers.

How to Use It:
- Describe what technical succession planning is and how it may differ from management succession planning.
- Send out the checksheet by email or else distribute it in a meeting and ask a group of managers to complete the checklist.
- Ask those who complete the checksheet to add up their "yes" and "no" check marks.
- Feed back to managers how they rated the organization's technical succession planning practices.
- Ask managers what they believe should be done to address the technical succession planning needs of the organization.

(Continued)

Exhibit 11.3 *(Continued)*

Use this checksheet to assess the status of the organization's technical succession planning practices. For each issue listed and described in the left column below, assess the current status by marking a number in the right column. Use this scale: **1 = Not at all adequate; 2 = Hardly adequate; 3 = Adequate; 4 = Good; 5 = Excellent**

Assessing the Organization's Technical Succession Planning Process

	Not at all			Excellent	

How well is the organization

		Not at all				Excellent
1.	*Making the commitment:* Decide that there is need to identify and capture specialized knowledge and institutional memory before those people who possess that knowledge leave the organization due to retirement, disability, or death.	1	2	3	4	5
2.	*Clarifying* **what** *work processes are key to achieving the organization's mission and strategic objectives.*	1	2	3	4	5
3.	*Clarifying who possess specialized knowledge about the work processes.*	1	2	3	4	5
4.	*Clarifying* **how** *those work processes are performed by the best, most experienced performers.*	1	2	3	4	5
5.	*Capturing and distilling the specialized knowledge about those work processes that is possessed by those possessing specialized knowledge.*	1	2	3	4	5
6.	*Considering how to maintain and transmit specialized knowledge and who needs it to ensure the efficient and effective continuity of operations.*	1	2	3	4	5
7.	*Continuously assessing knowledge gaps, evaluating the action strategies taken to address them, and the results achieved.*	1	2	3	4	5

Scoring

Add up your scores and place them in the box at right.

Scoring the Tool

If your score is 35–25:	Congratulations. Your effort is pretty good.
If your score is 24–19:	The organization needs to devote more time and attention to this issue.
If your score is 18–0:	Stop. Look. Listen: Focus attention on the issue immediately!

Source: William J. Rothwell

This checksheet provides a complementary check on the organization's readiness to undertake succession. It is aimed at the line manager of a technical or professional department who should be examining whether the department has adequately planned for replacing critically needed expertise or competence. With many organizations facing the loss of experienced professionals due to large-scale retirements of the baby boomers, this tool may be especially useful.

The next tool is not an assessment tool but a template that can follow and build upon the assessment results. The Business Case for Succession Tool (presented as Exhibit 11.4) offers a template for laying out the business rationale for succession and

Exhibit 11.4 The Business Case for Succession Tool

What It Is:

- A construction kit to craft a business case that creates a compelling sense of urgency for action to establish or enhance succession management.

When to Use It:

- The business case can help you
  Provide a clear link between business drivers and priority gaps in succession management. Create a compelling rationale for initiating improvements in how talent is managed for the future

How to Use It:

- Draw the Grid Below
  —*Step 1*

Business Drivers and Implications		But,
Current state		which produces
Risks and costs		On the other hand, if
Future state		which would produce
Benefits		Therefore,
First steps		

—*Step 2* In the second column, next to each heading, write down the key elements that your audience will need in the business case.

Business Drivers and Implications: The talent implications of key business and organization trends and dynamics.

(*Continued*)

Exhibit 11.4 (*Continued*)

Current State: Elements of the existing situation that create issues for the organization in securing the talent needed for the future, including organizational readiness factors. This could include existing talent gaps, inadequate systems (e.g., processes, tools, capabilities), and unsupportive culture.

Risks and Costs: The practical, negative effects of the current state and the result of continuing to do nothing to address the issues identified.

Future State: The new, rectified situation that can be envisioned and achieved—if only a solution could be found.

Benefits: The practical, positive effects of achieving the future state.

First Steps: Initial steps that would enable the organization to begin to close the gap between the current and future state, including the involvement necessary to take those steps, particularly from your audience.

—*Step 3* Reading across from column 2 to 3, row by row, and rewriting segments as necessary, construct your business case as a single paragraph.

—*Step 4* Expand the paragraph to the appropriate style and format—multiple pages, bullet points, notes for a conversation, whichever communication channel best suits your audience and your needs.

---

utilizing the information that may have emerged from the Readiness Assessment. It could form the basis for a mission statement about the goals and intent of the succession system. It is meant to help you think through why this initiative is urgent and important to the goals of the organization.

12

DEVELOPMENT TOOLS

Creating Development Plans w/o Focused Resources

Whether a succession system is developmental or not is the biggest decision that influences how the system is perceived by the participants in it. It is at the crux of how the system connects to the organization's values and culture. Using succession as the powerful driver of a development process takes true commitment and resources. It is worse to create a set of development plans with no resources to take them forward than to avoid development planning completely.

All of the research on adult learning in organizations points to the need to vary the learning approach and to build in time for on-the-job application in order to promote retention. This does not mean that every organization should, or can, offer every type of development opportunity. It does mean that the manner in which the different types of learning are tied together is essential to effectiveness, and that good developmental succession planning should consider how individual executives learn and develop best. The decision may often be to put the executive into a stretch assignment that takes him out of his comfort zone not only in terms of the assignment itself but also in terms of the type of learning involved. Here's an example: An individual may be most comfortable with evaluating a business from an analytical point of view, immersed in numbers and figures. It may be useful for her to attempt to construct a portrait of the business by focusing intensively on the people—doing in-depth interviews, for example, rather than relying on financials.

We present four development tools in this chapter. The first two—the Development Initiatives Checklist and William Rothwell's Clarifying the Goals of a Talent Management Program—are aimed at helping sort out the types of development initiatives available. The third development tool is Linkage's Developing a Job Profile. The final tool presented is the Individual Development Checklist.

The Development Initiatives Checklist (Exhibit 12.1) and Clarifying the Goals of a Talent Management Program (Exhibit 12.2) present an approach to making choices about where the focus of a talent and succession management system should be and how it will include development.

Exhibit 12.1 The Development Initiatives Checklist

What It Is:
- A comprehensive list of best-practice approaches to driving development used by leading organizations worldwide

When to Use It:
- When you need to drive a discussion on development alternatives
- To help move thinking on development beyond classroom-based approaches

How to Use It:
- Use this as a quick survey with senior management or stakeholders in the succession process to determine the current strengths and gaps in the development system and where you want to concentrate your development resources.

Development Initiative	Currently Using?		Priority (H,M,L)	Application in Succession Process
	Yes	No		
360 assessment & feedback				
Exposure to key executives				
Exposure to strategy planning process				
Cross-functional rotation				
Global rotations				
International project work				
Action learning programs				
Coaching (internal or external)				
Mentoring (informal or formal)				
Individual development plans				
Informal coaching and mentoring				
Internal case studies				
Leadership development workshops and institutes				
Leveraging internal personnel as faculty				
Executive MBA program				

Exhibit 12.2 Clarifying the Goals of a Talent Management Program

What It Is:

- Poor goal setting is a common reason why many talent management programs are not as successful as they should be. Each manager believes that his or her own goals are the most important, and there are actually many goals that an organization could achieve from a talent management program.

- This tool permits senior managers to begin to clarify what the senior executive team desires as goals for the talent management program. That, in turn, provides a solid foundation for subsequent measurement efforts for talent management. After all, if nobody is sure of the goals, then it is not possible to measure the success of the talent management program.

When to Use It:

- Use this assessment instrument for opening a conversation among senior managers about the desired results for a talent management program.

- Senior executives and those otherwise charged with decision-making responsibility for talent management programs.

How to Use It:

- Explain to senior managers that talent management programs cannot be "all things to all people" and that priority setting is necessary.

- Emphasize that, without discussion, senior managers may actually differ in their expectations for a talent management program.

- Ask senior managers to complete the instrument before a meeting and return the instrument to one person.

- Ask the administrator—that is, the person who receives completed instruments— to compile the scores from all the managers and be prepared to feed the scores back to managers in a meeting.

- Once managers have seen how they collectively scored the goals for the talent management program, ask them to agree on the top three priorities and why those priorities are important.

Directions: Review the possible goals for a talent management program listed in the left column below. Then, in the right column, rate *how important meeting that goal is to your organization.* Use the following scale: **0 = Not applicable; 1 = Not at all important; 2 = Somewhat important; 3 = Important; 4 = Very important.**

	Goal	How Important Is Meeting This Goal to Your Organization?				
		Not Applicable	*Not at All Important*	*Somewhat Important*	*Important*	*Very Important*
1	Provide increased opportunities for "high potential" workers	0	1	2	3	4
2	Identify "replacement needs" as a means of targeting necessary training, employee education, and employee development	0	1	2	3	4

(Continued)

Exhibit 12.2 (*Continued*)

Goal	How Important Is Meeting This Goal to Your Organization?				
	Not Applicable	Not at All Important	Somewhat Important	Important	Very Important
3 Increase the talent pool of promotable employees	0	1	2	3	4
4 Contribute to implementing the organization's strategic business plan	0	1	2	3	4
5 Help individuals realize their career plans within the organization	0	1	2	3	4
6 Untap the potential for intellectual capital in the organization	0	1	2	3	4
7 Encourage the advancement of diverse groups	0	1	2	3	4
8 Improve employees' ability to respond to changing environmental demands	0	1	2	3	4
9 Improve employee morale	0	1	2	3	4
10 Cope with the effects of voluntary separation programs	0	1	2	3	4
11 Other (*Please list them and rate them:*)	0	1	2	3	4

Prioritizing the Goals

Please note that not all goals can be achieved. So, what are the top three most important goals (from those listed in the left column above) to be met by this program, in your opinion, and why are they important? Please list them below.

Exhibit 12.2 (*Continued*)

Goal (*Please list them in order of importance where 1 = most important*)		Why Is It Important?
1		
2		
3		

Source: William J. Rothwell

The Developing a Job Profile Tool (Exhibit 12.3), is helpful in making the connection from assessment of candidates to the practical questions of how to structure their jobs to achieve both learning and results.

The tool, which is based on collaborative work between Linkage and Patricia McLagan, is relevant at both the organizational and individual levels of the succession process. It provides a guide to thinking through the critical work context and customer issues impacting any job or function. It also demands that one define the outputs or results expected before determining needed competencies. Too many of the competency models developed skip this critical step of determining the relationship of the required competencies to actual results. This is needed if the job profile and the succession process are designed to connect to performance. Otherwise, while the competencies defined may be desirable ones, their expected relationship to driving actual performance and results may be unclear. Succession planning involves making suppositions around which competencies, experiences, and abilities will drive future performance.

Exhibit 12.3 The Developing a Job Profile Tool

What Is This Tool?

- This tool will help you connect a team's daily work to the organization's strategic needs and context.
- It consists of a useful structure for identifying the context, customers, output, and competencies relating to a job.

When Do I Use It?

- When you need to establish a team's performance framework
- When you need to clarify the team's contributions in alignment with the strategic direction of the organization
- When you need to determine what the team is responsible for producing—for whom, to what end, and at what expected level of quality
- When you need to identify competencies needed within the work team

How Do I Use It?

Step 1: Review the elements of the job profile shown in Figure 12.1 and review the explanation of each box.

Figure 12.1 Elements of a Job Profile

Work Context	Customers
• Determine key external and internal conditions driving performance.	• Determine key receivers of work.
Outputs	**Competencies**
• Determine key work to be produced for customers.	• Determine key competencies required to produce outputs at superior levels.

Explanation of the Boxes

Box 1: Work Context These are the conditions that will affect the team's work—the external and internal forces that affect the work of the team as well as the goals and results that the team needs to impact. Refer to your long-term goals, and add all the changes in technology, markets, work conditions, business strategies, work processes, and so forth that will likely impact your team.

Box 2: Customers Who will receive products, services, information, decisions, support, plans, and so forth from the team during the next performance period? List these internal and external customers in the Customers box of the job profile. Try to list only five to seven critical customers for the team. Do not list yourself unless your team is actually paid to provide value-adding products or services to you.

Box 3: Outputs Keeping the identified performance period in mind, ask, "What will our customers need at the end of this time?" List all the routine outputs *and* any new outputs needed to support business strategies and plans (refer to the team's context statement to define new outputs needed). They should be outputs that require team cooperation, not just individual contributions.

Box 4: Competencies Determine what it will take for team members to produce the outputs at a superior level. Identify the knowledge, skills, and commitments required to perform those activities that result in the outputs.

Exhibit 12.3 (*Continued*)

Helpful Hints

A job profile helps you and your team to stay future-focused by emphasizing the changing nature of your work circumstances. Two critical factors that the Work Context box calls attention to are:

1. *Forces:* Driving and restraining forces affecting the business that will impact your work.
2. *Goals/Results to Impact:* Team performance goals that will contribute to the achievement of the organization's overall strategic goals

Thinking through each of these in turn will help you understand the changing context of your work and adjust accordingly.

If possible, talk with key stakeholders about the items you included in the Work Context box. Now and in the future, stay informed about the forces impacting your team's work and the strategic goals you must support. Be sure you understand the relationship among overarching strategic goals, your unit's goals, and your team's goals.

Step 2: Now review the prototype job profile presented in Figure 12.2, as well as the accompanying quality requirements and behavioral indicators presented in Tables 12.1a and 12.1b.

Figure 12.2 Prototype Job Profile: Maître D' at the All-American Restaurant

Work Context	Customers
Forces • Increasing variety of menu items • Growing family diner population • Shrinking profit margins **Goals/Results to Impact** • Improved customer satisfaction • Increase returning customers • Increase volume of patrons by 10%	• Patrons/Diners • Owner • Waitstaff
Outputs	**Competencies**
• Complaints handled • Exit greetings • Feedback to chef • Greeted customers • Menus to customers • Mood atmosphere • Reservation list • Seated customers • Valet service attained • Waiting list • Wine cellar maintenance	• Conflict management techniques knowledge • Coordination • Customer knowledge • Judgment • Listening skills • Organizational skills • Product and service knowledge • Verbal communication skills

(Continued)

Exhibit 12.3 (*Continued*)

Table 12.1a Quality Requirements for Maître D' Job

Selected Outputs	*Quality Requirements*
Reservation List	• Accurate (correct name, time, number of people in party, and any special requests/needs) • Timely (written in reservation book at time that reservation is made) • Quantity (number of reservations made equal to ability of scheduled staff to handle, appropriate number of "over books" made to account for no-shows)
Menus to Customers	• Quality (given to women first, slowly handed, depleted menu items communicated, specials noted) • Timely (given *at* time of seating)
Complaints Handled	• Timely (within 10 minutes of recognition of situation) • Quality (meeting satisfaction of the customer)

Table 12.1b Behavioral Indicators for Maître D' Job

Selected Competencies	*Behavioral Indicators*
Listening Skills	• Utilizes nonverbals to signal that he or she is listening • Paraphrases to ensure correct understanding • Gives undivided concentration to what is being said to increase understanding
Product and Service Knowledge	• Checks with chef on daily specials and depleted items • Asks waitstaff what items have been favorites of patrons • Describes any product in detail upon request
Judgment	• Understands impact of decisions on customers and wait staff • Handles situations by applying appropriate criteria

Step 3: Now, using the form presented in Figure 12.3, complete a job profile for each member of your team.

Exhibit 12.3 (*Continued*)

Figure 12.3   Job Profile Form

Team: _____

Performance Period: _____

Work Context	Customers
Forces: Goals/Results to Impact:	
Outputs	**Competencies**

The last tool is the Individual Development Plan Creation Checklist (Exhibit 12.4), which we have developed at Linkage. It contains a form on which the employee can identify goals and strategies in preparation for the development meeting, as well as a form on which to record the results of a six-month follow-up. The individual development plan (IDP) should raise issues around how the work of the participant will be sponsored and should encourage the manager to discuss how the participant will deepen and enlarge their own network. The development process should also consider how any development strategies will also drive business impact. Obviously, if the IDP is tied into a business impact or if the learning and competence development involved has a clear business connection, it will increase the likelihood of support and follow-through. We also refer you to Chapter One, by Phil Harkins, on "A New Methodology: Succession, Progression, and Development." In this chapter, Phil presents tools that strongly tie the succession strategy to the business vision and goals and will help you think through the critical capabilities and candidates to focus on as well as the highest impact development options.

Exhibit 12.4 Individual Development Plan Creation Checklist

What It Is:

- A set of forms to organize the initial development planning meeting as well as a three- or six-month follow-up.

When to Use It:

- The Individual Development Plan form will best be used as preparation prior to the meetings between the employee and his or her manager. Other stakeholders, such as the next level manager or the human resources professional, could also sign up to sponsor the development plan.
- The summary format can be used at any meaningful time interval (three months, six months, etc.) to evaluate the progress being made on the development plans.

How to Use It:

- Development planning must be systematic and involve more than structured formal classroom learning. This IDP format encourages the use of multiple approaches to learning and growth. It should be used to challenge the thinking about how and when development will occur and what supports are needed.
- The summary format is designed to ensure a thorough and thoughtful development process over time. As research has shown, development planning without follow-up has little or no chance to take hold.

  ☐ Identify success factors that need current improvement; make goals specific, measurable, and challenging.

  ☐ Complete the IDP Development Plan (Figure 12.4), remembering the following:

  ○ Discern and prioritize specific goals.

  ○ Decide how these goals will be accomplished.

  ○ Identify resources to supplement improvement.

  ○ Consider possible obstacles and how to manage these obstacles.

  ○ Contract with partners for constructive feedback.

  ○ Develop indicators of success and evaluate progress.

  ○ Determine the specific impact improved performance will have on the business.

  ○ Commit to following through with the process.

  ☐ Review the learning process to make sure processes fit the working conditions to promote the most successful outcome.

  ☐ Incorporate actions that encourage successful learning and achievement of goals.

Exhibit 12.4 (*Continued*)

Figure 12.4 Individual Development Plan Worksheet

Name (print): _____ Manager: _____	IDP Start Date:_____ IDP Review Date:_____ End Date: _____

Development Goal

Write your Development Goal using a complete sentence. Do not use bullet points. One goal per form.

_____

_____

_____

List capabilities related to your goal	Identify business goals and projects related to these capabilities and your development goal
_____ _____	_____ _____

Development Strategies

On-the-job learning assignments and opportunities	Progress/review dates	Formal/structured training, program, education	Progress/review dates

Anticipated Results & Benefits

What results do you expect—with customers, peers, direct reports, and managers—from learning and applying your new capabilities to the job?

Resources

List resource (time, people, etc.) that may be needed to help you accomplish your development goal

Employee's signature:	Date submitted:
Manager's signature:	Date approved:

(*Continued*)

Exhibit 12.4 *(Continued)*

The Individual Development Summary Form (Figure 12.5) can be used to record the results of a follow-up meeting.

Figure 12.5 Individual Development Summary Form

Individual Development Summary Form		
Name:	**Reason(s) for Selection:**	**Development Successes**
	"Best of your Best":	Assignments, projects
	Next in line for promotion:	Mentoring
	Most critical project:	Executive coaching
Title/Grade:	Best long term potential:	One-on-one coaching
	Other:	Increased decision making/delegation
	Comments:	External development assignments
		Programs/workshops
Manager:		Other:
		Comments:
What is working?		What is not working?
Help needed and source:		
Comments:		

Exhibit 12.4 (*Continued*)

General Discussion Topics	
Item	*Comment, Question, Other*
Assignments, projects:	
Mentoring:	
Executive coaching:	
One-on-one coaching:	
Increased decision Making/delegation:	
External development assignments:	
Programs/workshops:	
SVP development process:	
Other: development "Best Practices":	

13

EVALUATION TOOLS

The Measure and Learn Phase

Succession systems should be continuously evaluated and improved as conditions and demands change for the organization. A big part of measuring and learning needs to be the connection between the succession system and the other parts of the human resource management system. We have developed a Retention Survey: Self-Assessment (presented as Exhibit 13.1), which could be used as a self-assessment or as a more comprehensive resource. This survey is connected to the Retention Analysis Worksheet (Exhibit 13.2), which aims at six key considerations to drive effective organizational strategies around retention.

The Measures of Effectiveness Tool (Exhibit 13.3) provides a checklist that is aimed at the evaluation side of the succession process. It captures many of the typical measures of the impact of succession. It should prompt the consultant to think about whether succession is defined in a way that encompasses broader human resource goals such as diversity and how the succession process relates to selection and performance systems.

We have provided two tools to examine the comprehensiveness of your overall succession effort. The first is a helpful form entitled the Top-Level Succession Plan Review (Exhibit 13.4), which captures all the elements in the succession process, points out key factors that should have been included in each of these elements, and allows the practitioner to pinpoint anything that may have been missed. This tool is meant for the development professional who needs to plan for all of the detailed

Exhibit 13.1 Retention Survey: Self-Assessment

√hat It Is:

- This survey is aimed at looking at whether certain specific practices are in place that can help with the retention of key employees.

When to Use It:

- The survey is best used before moving into planning for development activities and how the succession process will be tied into the larger talent planning and human resource management systems.

How to Use It:

- This informal survey can be tailored to meet your organization's needs. It provides systematic data which could be shared with a management team that is planning for its talent and succession needs. As such, it should be administered to the senior team and at least one level of managers below them.

1 = Disagree, 4 = Agree

Strategy				
The organization clearly communicates its vision for the future.	1	2	3	4
My individual work goals are aligned with broader organizational goals.	1	2	3	4
Strategic goals set by different units are aligned within the organization.	1	2	3	4
Architecture				
The organization gives employees opportunities to offer feedback to leadership.	1	2	3	4
The organization informs employees about its goals, plans, and strategies.	1	2	3	4
Divisional heads regularly meet to coordinate the efforts of different functions in the organization.	1	2	3	4
Work Processes				
The organization provides clear and challenging work goals.	1	2	3	4
The organization utilizes measurable performance standards.	1	2	3	4
The organization provides flexible work assignments to accommodate employee work/life demands.	1	2	3	4

Exhibit 13.1 (*Continued*)

1 = Disagree, 4 = Agree

Work Processes				
The organization offers services or programs to help take care of errands that I may need to run during the workday.	1	2	3	4
The organization utilizes clear standards for effective project management.	1	2	3	4
The organization regularly revisits key processes for continual improvement.	1	2	3	4
People Practices				
The organization trains its managers how to coach employees.	1	2	3	4
The organization has processes in place to encourage feedback between peers, subordinates, and managers.	1	2	3	4
The organization offers pay and benefits that match or exceed that of competitors.	1	2	3	4
The organization links incentives or bonuses to organizational performance.	1	2	3	4
The organization empowers its managers to immediately reward strong individual employee performance.	1	2	3	4
The organization publicly supports and praises high performers.	1	2	3	4
Culture/Branding				
The organization only hires people that demonstrate its corporate values.	1	2	3	4
The organization clearly defines its values, beliefs, and principles.	1	2	3	4
The organization creates an environment where experimentation and mistakes are valued as long as learning takes place.	1	2	3	4
The organization provides accurate information to employees, regardless of whether the information is positive or negative.	1	2	3	4
The organization allows employees to participate when making important decisions.	1	2	3	4

Exhibit 13.2 Retention Analysis Worksheet

Question	Strategies for Improvement
Why do people stay?	What can you do to maximize and leverage these factors?
Why have people left?	What can you do to find out the impact of these reasons on current employees?
What would cause people to consider leaving?	What can you do to fill the gaps and reduce potential turnover?

Exhibit 13.3 The Measures of Effectiveness Tool

What It Is:

- This tool will help organizations to identify a high-potential talent pool. It can be used to set periodic reviews and monitor progress and also to review the potential-related development activities and programs.

When To Use It:

- This tool should be used to check on the development progress of the talent pool. It can be used to build accountability for the high-potential employees.

How to Use It:

Result Measures	Current State	Needed Improvement
Bench strength: two or more candidates each in "ready now" and "future" categories		
Percentage of women and minority promotions versus percentage in pool		
Percentage of women and minority successors		
Retention rate of successors		
Percentage of key jobs filled internally		
Promotion rate of successors		
Success rate of those promoted as identified successors		
Cost to fill key roles		

Process Measures	Current State	Needed Improvement
Perceived fairness of the process by those identified as successors and others		
User-friendliness of processes and tools		
Quality of information available in successors and other talent		
Quality and success of development plans		
Senior management involvement in and support for the system		
Level of development activity and learning of successors		
Deployability: "Ready now" total includes many different individuals (not same few)		
Time to fill open positions		

Exhibit 13.4 The Top-Level Succession Plan Review

What It Is:

- This tool provides a seven-step outline of the major activities and decision points required to develop and implement a succession management program. While specific implementation needs will vary depending on which process you already have in place and decisions you may have made, the tool provides suggestions as a checklist for building your own implementation plan.

When to Use It:

- While this checklist is helpful in completing a detailed implementation plan early in the succession process, it may also be used to evaluate whether certain steps have been completed or need to be reworked later on in the process.

How to Use It:

- This tool is intended for the succession project planning team to use to focus their activities. It should be connected to a timeline so that management will fully understand the time required to roll out the succession effort.

   1. *Develop Architecture and Design*
      - ❑ Scale and scope
      - ❑ Objectives, principles, and values
      - ❑ Stakeholders
      - ❑ Target roles
      - ❑ Process, tools, and capabilities
      - ❑ Integration
      - ❑ Measures

   2. *Develop Overall Implementation Plan*
      - ❑ Master schedule and project plan (for company, division/unit, etc.)
      - ❑ Resources required
      - ❑ Instructions and guidelines
      - ❑ Communications plan

   3. *Hold Executive Meeting to Answer Questions and Provide Direction*
      - ❑ Overview of the process and schedule
      - ❑ Build relationships
      - ❑ Gauge commitment and involvement
      - ❑ Improve quality of pre-work and submission
      - ❑ "Assist" with assessments and submissions as needed
      - ❑ Answer questions and head-off potential issues
      - ❑ Review "next steps"

Exhibit 13.4 (*Continued*)

4. *Assess Bench Strength*
- ❑ Executive-level discussions
- ❑ Assess performance
- ❑ Assess potential
- ❑ Determine readiness for key roles
- ❑ Identify critical gaps between future talent needs and current talent
- ❑ Assemble information for management review

5. *Roll-Up Information*
- ❑ Direct reports
- ❑ High potential individuals and readiness
- ❑ Strengths, promotion recommendations
- ❑ Development requirements and action steps
- ❑ Successors and timeframes for promotions
- ❑ Diversity/mix percentage
- ❑ Expatriate/international assignments

6. *Identify Risks*
- ❑ Lack of replacements/successors for key roles
- ❑ Potential turnover
- ❑ "Fit" problems
- ❑ Talent "blocks"
- ❑ Senior members not committed to process

7. *Identify Opportunities*
- ❑ People who can play multiple roles
- ❑ Deep "bench strength" areas
- ❑ Key mentors/talent developers

steps involved in the succession process. The second tool, from William Rothwell, provides a method for rating your organization against the best practices in succession management. Entitled Rating Your Organization against Best Practices in Succession Planning and Management (Exhibit 13.5), it can help drive a management group discussion on how well the organization's approach measures up to best practice.

In summary, evaluation must focus on the impact and comprehensiveness of the succession process as well as the depth and

Exhibit 13.5 Rating Your Organization Against Best Practices in Succession Planning and Management

What It Is:

- *Succession planning* is, quite literally, planning for the continuity of management talent. A succession planning program is thus focused as much around developing people for future opportunities as it is for replacing retiring managers. This checksheet allows users to rate their organizations against best practices. It should be able to be completed in 10 minutes or less.

When to Use It:

- Use this checksheet as a starting point for opening a conversation about how well the managers of an organization are managing their succession planning program.
- Ask senior managers to complete the checksheet and then feed it back for a group discussion and for planning improvement efforts.

How to Use It:

- Describe what succession planning is and how it may differ from replacement planning.
- Send out the checksheet by e-mail or else distribute it in a meeting and ask a group of managers to complete it.
- Ask those who complete the checksheet to add up their "yes" and "no" check marks.
- Feed back to managers how they rated the organization's succession planning practices.
- Ask managers what they believe should be done to improve the succession planning program of the organization.

Directions: For each item listed in the left column below, check a box in the right column to indicate whether your organization has addressed the item for purposes of the succession planning and management program.

For Succession Planning and Management, has your organization:	Yes ✓	No ✓
1 Clarified *why* a succession planning and management program is necessary based on an "assessment or risk" (how many retirements are expected over what time span?) and business continuity/growth requirements?		

Exhibit 13.5 (*Continued*)

For Succession Planning and Management, has your organization:	Yes ✓	No ✓
2 Clarified the *purpose* of the succession planning and management program in writing, having gotten agreement from the CEO and other senior leaders on what that purpose is?		
3 Clarified the *exact role* that the CEO wishes to play in the succession planning and management program (ranging from "total hands off" to "total hands on")?		
4 Established *clear priorities and/or measurable program objectives* so that the succession planning and management program does not try to be "all things to all people"?		
5 *Targeted groups or individuals to be served* by the succession planning and management program and *identified best-in-class performers* in the organization?		
6 *Established blueprints for the people of the future* through the development of a competency model for each targeted group?		
7 Integrated performance *management/appraisal* with the competency model(s) for targeted groups?		
8 Prepared a *flexible action plan* to guide implementation of the succession planning and management program with the recognition in mind that a "total system rollout" cannot occur at lightning speed?		
9 Established a *regular review schedule* to examine results of the succession planning and management program?		
10 Established a system for preparing *individual development plans* to guide the systematic preparation of talent in the organization?		
11 Created the means by which to *assess individuals against the competencies necessary at higher levels* through systematic, culture-specific 360-degree assessments, assessment centers, or other means that will avoid picking people for the future who are just clones of incumbents?		
12 Chosen appropriate *competency-building work experiences* that will build bench strength with individuals while also, at the same time, getting work accomplished?		

(*Continued*)

Exhibit 13.5 (Continued)

For Succession Planning and Management, has your organization:	Yes ✓	No ✓
13	Established a means to *reward executives for "people development"* and *hold people accountable* for implementation of individual development plans?		
14	Selected *appropriate software/technological assistance* to support the needs of the succession planning and management program?		

Scoring

(Add up the "yes" and "no" boxes and then insert the sums where indicated at right. Obviously, the more "yes" boxes your organization has, the closer your organization is aligned to best practice in succession planning and management.)	*Number of "Yes" Boxes*	*Number of "No" Boxes*

Scoring the Tool

If your score is 14–10:	**Congratulations. Your effort is pretty good and aligns well to best practice.**
If your score is 9–6:	**The organization needs to devote more time and attention to the succession program to bring it into alignment with best practice.**
If your score is 5 or below:	**Stop. Look. Listen: Focus attention on improving the succession program immediately!**

Source: William J. Rothwell

quality of the development experiences and follow through at the individual and group levels.

While use of these tools does not guarantee success, they will help you to keep on track and continuously improve your process.

Part Four

RESOURCE GUIDE

RESOURCES

Resource guides aimed specifically at developmental ideas and suggestions for leaders and executives can be a helpful tool in succession planning. First, they organize topics and concepts in a clean, concise manner; and connect them to leadership skills and competencies that executives need. We strongly encourage practitioners to use the best of these guides from Linkage, CCL, PDI, and other firms, as they are a cost effective way to build a library of development ideas, both formal (classes, books, and so on), and on the job. This particular resource guide is especially useful because not only does it provide relevant readings, but includes software and upcoming conferences as well. Each source is annotated with the main purpose and content of the source, so the reader can quickly see if that source is worth pursuing further.

This resource guide is designed to help business professionals—from the human resources generalist to the chief executive officer—gather and utilize a variety of detailed, in-depth information on succession planning. It includes books, articles, Web sites, software, videos, and future conferences that focus on the best ways for a company to develop, utilize, and maintain a successful succession plan.

Books

Grow Your Own Leaders: How to Identify, Develop, and Retain Leadership Talent

William C. Byham, Audrey B. Smith, and Matthew J. Paese
Prentice Hall (2002)

This book covers every phase of executive development and succession, introducing high-impact no-bureaucracy techniques for succession planning (SP). It is designed for tomorrow's companies and future leaders looking to implement an SP system. It discusses best practices for identifying "high potentials" in an organization. This book will give you a system for looking inside your organization to find leadership potential, prepare leaders quickly, and deploy them as new leadership challenges emerge.

The War for Talent

Ed Michaels, Helen Handfield-Jones, and Beth Axelrod
Harvard Business School Press (2001)

This book consists of extensive research that helps provide a quantitative understanding of what does and doesn't make a difference in building a strong talent pool. The case studies included in this book provide a qualitative understanding of how companies make great talent management happen. This book will help companies build executive and managerial talent and long-term recruiting strategies.

Effective Succession Planning: Ensuring Leadership Continuity and Building Talent from Within

William J. Rothwell
AMACOM (2001)

This book provides in-depth and complete information to help you establish, revitalize, or evaluate a succession planning and management program for your firm. It includes case studies, self-assessments, planning guides, and more to help you accurately gauge your succession planning requirements. It will serve as a guide to help you determine how your organization is handling succession planning and management.

The Talent Management Handbook: Creating Organizational Excellence by Identifying, Developing, and Promoting Your Best People

Lance A. Berger and Dorothy R. Berger
McGraw-Hill (2004)

This book discusses how to systematically identify, keep, develop, and promote your organization's best people. It explains how to align your company's people with the current and future needs of the organization by placing employees in positions that maximize their value. Also discusses how to allocate training resources to employees based on actual and/or potential contribution to organizational excellence.

Career Planning and Succession Management: Developing Your Organization's Talent—For Today and Tomorrow

William J. Rothwell, Robert D. Jackson, Shaun C. Knight, and John E. Lindholm Praeger (2005)

This book features numerous diagnostics, checklists, and other interactive elements that demonstrate how to create that crucial link between succession and career development programs. Also discusses how to develop organizational talent from the bottom up and top down simultaneously. It can be used as a guide for leaders and human resource professionals looking to align individual and organizational goals to ensure their economic future.

Succession Planning and Management: A Guide to Organizational Systems and Practices

David Berke
Center for Creative Leadership (2005)

This book discusses linkages between succession and development, and considers representative literature on chief executive officer succession, high potentials, succession systems and architecture. Organizations can use this book for conceptualizing, planning, and implementing effective succession systems.

Growing Your Company's Leaders: How Great Organizations Use Succession Management to Sustain Competitive Advantage

Robert M. Fulmer and Jay Alden Conger
AMACOM (2004)

This book presents the results of a benchmarking study of six global companies that have created strong succession planning systems. Discusses special roles executives and human resource managers play in succession planning systems, as well as how an organization defines and identifies talent for crucial positions.

Succession Planning: Take Two

Sandra Hastings
ASTD Press (2004)

This book presents a four-phase succession planning model for establishing the scope, creation, implementation, and evaluation of the plan. It discusses preparing a plan that gets the right people into the right jobs at the right time.

The Leadership Pipeline: How to Build the Leadership Powered Company

Ram Charan, Stephen Drotter, and James Noel
Jossey-Bass (2001)

This book provides readers with a proven method for building a leadership pipeline by defining six critical leadership passages, assessing competence and performance at each passage, and planning leadership development in a way that addresses the unique challenge of each passage. It gives managers and human resource professionals the framework, tools, and language they need to help leaders at every level reach their full potential.

ESOP and ESOP Workbook: The Ultimate Instrument in Succession Planning

Robert A. Frisch
John Wiley & Sons (2002)

This book contains forms, checklists, and step-by-step instructions for choosing and implementing an ESOP and succession planning system, as well as useful information for financial advisors and life insurance agents who need to know about ESOPs for their business. It is also designed to help the corporate owner, financial officer, certified public accountant, and attorney determine whether an ESOP is appropriate for meeting a company's objectives and, if so, how to successfully implement a suitable succession planning system.

Business Succession Planning

Paul Winn
Dearborn Financial Publishing (2000)

This book discusses reasons why it is important to prepare for business succession planning and transferring ownership. It also discusses ways to replace the loss of key people and reorganizing the business for the future.

Making a Leadership Change: How Organizations and Leaders Can Handle Leadership Transitions Successfully

Thomas North Gilmore
Authors Choice Press (2003)

This book offers sound advice for executives and managers taking over new positions and for organizations undergoing leadership changes. It provides practical guidance on all phases of the leadership transition process and details how a company can minimize the risks of making changes at the top.

The Executive Director's Survival Guide: Thriving as a Nonprofit Leader

Mim Carlson and Margaret Donohoe
Jossey-Bass (2002)

This book focuses on executive directors in nonprofit organizations and the best ways they can lead organizational change. The book states that the executive director must examine the organization's effectiveness and his or her own personal performance to be successful. It also discusses strategies for changing an organization's culture to where it needs to be in order for the organization to be successful.

The First 90 Days: Critical Success Strategies for New Leaders at All Levels

Michael Watkins
Harvard Business School Press (2003)

This book discusses ways for taking charge quickly and effectively during critical career transition periods. It is based on three years of research into leadership transitions at all levels and hands-on work designing transition programs for top companies. It discusses a number of important elements, including how to balance personal and professional demands during the transition.

Planning for Succession: A Toolkit for Board Members and Staff of Nonprofit Arts Organizations

Merianne Liteman
Illinois Arts Alliance Foundation (2003)

This workbook-style toolkit includes guidelines, checklists, best practices, and frequently asked questions for arts groups and other nonprofits that are facing— or should be thinking about—executive succession. It is a valuable resource for board members and others involved in arts and nonprofit organizations, as well as educators, funders, and those interested in the concept of leadership succession.

The Strategic Development of Talent

William J. Rothwell
HRD Press, Inc. (2004)

This book discusses the importance and purpose of talent development in relation to strategic business planning and human resource planning. It explains how to accurately compare actual to desired knowledge and skills and how to choose and implement organizational strategy for the development of talent. It also provides an instrument to assess the competencies of stakeholders in the talent development effort.

Talent Management Systems: Best Practices in Technology Solutions for Recruitment, Retention, and Workforce Planning

Allan Schweyer
John Wiley & Sons (2004)

This book discusses the best ways for companies to implement technology into their talent management processes. Allan Schweyer is a leader and respected author in this area.

Keeping the People Who Keep You in Business: 24 Ways to Hang on to Your Most Valuable Talent

Leigh Branham
American Management Association (2000)

This book discusses ways managers can better retain their best employees, even suggesting that turnover is advantageous if it manages to keep your very best employees while weeding out poor performers. The author groups twenty-four retention strategies into four key components, including being a company people want to work for and hiring the right people in the first place.

Practical Succession Management: How to Future-Proof Your Organisation

Andrew Munro
Gower Publishing Company (2005)

This book is intended for a number of business professionals including HR directors, resourcing and development professionals, and chief executive officers. It answers essential employee-related questions: *Who do we need, where do we need them, and when?* It includes a toolkit that has checklists that can be customized to a company's requirements.

Succession Management: A Guide for Your Journey to Best-Practice Processes

Darcy Lemons, Nadia Uddin, Wes Vestal, and Rachele Williams
American Productivity and Quality Center (2004)

This book explores initiating a succession management effort, performing a needs analysis, identifying talent, and other important areas. It uses examples from best-practice organizations and reveals how to identify and develop potential in employees, as well as how to retain existing employees.

Articles

"Ending the CEO Succession Crisis"

Ram Charan
Harvard Business Review (February 2005)

This article describes why CEO succession is broken in America, why top leaders fail in office, and why leadership pipelines are empty. It provides real-life examples to show you what works and what does not work for succession planning. It discusses aspects of CEO succession such as internal development programs, board supervision, and outside recruitment.

"How Strong Is Your Bench"

Jim Bolt
Fast Company (2004)

This article highlights survey findings to show company trends in executive and leadership development. It offers suggestions for investing in your company's future pertaining to concepts such as integrated talent management systems, working sessions, and reviewing and refining your development process.

"Matching People and Jobs"

Vivek Agrawal, James M. Manyika, and John E. Richards
McKinsey Quarterly (2003)

This article discusses pinpointing the people in your organization who do the best work and how to increase the value of your employees by increasing productivity of individual workers and utilizing the most effective technology. It also discusses the importance of anticipating your company's future workforce requirements.

"Nothing Succeeds Like Succession"

Thomas Wailgum
CIO magazine (May 2005)

This article is a case study on the succession planning process used by United Parcel Service (UPS). It identifies succession planning and employee development as integral parts of UPS's management system and how UPS utilizes a formal talent identification program.

"Most Major Corporations Unprepared for Potential Succession Needs, According to Global Survey of Recruiters"

PR Newswire (May 2005)

This article highlights results from a survey on succession planning taken by Executive Recruiter Index. It identifies succession planning mistakes such as lack of preparation, no formal evaluation processes, and overly rigid position specifications.

"75% of Companies Disregard CEO Exit Plans"

PR Newswire (July 2005)

This article states that the majority of companies do not have proper succession plans in place. It highlights results from a report on succession planning by Cutting Edge Information. One conclusion is that succession planning enhances operational performance.

"Workstream Succession Planning Solution Is Selected by IAC/InterActiveCorp to Support HR Planning Processes for Senior Management"

Business Wire (July 2005)

This article covers Workstream's newly selected succession planning solution to manage its HR planning processes. The solution also includes leadership development.

"John Hancock Launches Succession Planning Sales Toolkit"

PR Newswire (June 2005)

This article gives an overview of the kit, which contains resources to help advisors educate their clients about succession planning. The kit covers simple key-person insurance plans and more complex buy-sell arrangements.

"SuccessFactors Media Alert: Advice for HP's Board on Succession Planning"

Business Wire (February 2005)

This article illustrates five key guidelines for effective succession planning, including mapping your company's talent base and implementing succession planning at all levels of your company.

"Succession Planning . . . Organisational Evolution"

www.getfeedback.net (2003)

This article discusses the importance of both human resources and current leadership in an organization coming together to implement succession planning. It illustrates four good reasons for conducting a comprehensive succession planning process and six criteria for choosing the right employee to move up in management.

"HR Professionals Share Succession Planning Tips"

HRfocus (July 2005)

This article highlights responses from an *HRfocus* Succession Survey showing different approaches to succession planning, such as creating specific assessment and development plans for key talent and involving 360-degree feedback and executive coaching.

"Succession Planning Is Now Too Important for Partners to Put on the Back Burner"

Partner's Report for Law Firm Owners (March 2005)

This article discusses the significance of succession planning for law firms given an aging population of founding partners, changing firm structures, and staffing concerns. It suggests that a firm's succession plan address five elements, including economics and timing.

"Top Must-Haves for Succession Planning"

Law Office Management and Administration Report (February 2005)

This article states that succession planning is a necessity for law firms and lists key points to remember for succession planning, such as reevaluating and reassessing within the firm so leaders understand who is responsible for what.

"Nitty-Gritty Ideas for Succession Planning"

Accounting Office Management and Administration Report (June 2005)

This article discusses ways to make succession planning easier for CPA firms, such as a sound strategy and a market for the successors. This article also includes a succession planning case study on the firm Daszkal Bolton, LLP.

"Board Responsibility for CEO Succession Planning"

L. Edward Shaw
Aspen Publishers, Inc. (May 2005)

This article discusses the importance of utilizing succession planning early in order to choose a chief executive officer (CEO). It gives examples of companies that had problems with CEO selection due to an inadequate succession planning process. It suggests that a succession plan should cover unexpected developments such as death or early departure.

"Strategic Planning: Read This Before You Plan for Succession"

Accounting Office Management and Administration Report (June 2005)

This article previews a book by William Reeb on succession planning for CPA firms. Reeb emphasizes key areas such as operations, governance, accountability, marketing, and staff training that must be solidly in place before succession planning can begin. It includes highlights from a PCPS succession survey.

"Leveraging HR: How to Develop Leaders in 'Real Time'"

Linda Sharkey
Human Resources in the 21st Century (2003)

The writer of the article and a GE Financial Services employee discusses how GE implements internal coaching into the organizational structure. The article highlights a behavioral model that shows steps in the behavioral coaching process and explains how GE uses human resource professionals as leadership coaches.

"Knowledge Transfer: 12 Strategies for Succession Management"

William Rothwell
IPMA-HR News

This article outlines the most critical steps and strategies needed to develop an effective succession management system. It includes key learning points for top executives, managers, and employees at every level.

"Introducing Technical (Not Managerial) Succession Planning"

William Rothwell and S. Poduch
Public Personnel Management, 33:4 (2004)

This article examines technical succession planning and how it differs from managerial succession planning. It offers a case study that illustrates how one government agency addresses this issue.

"Expanding the Value of Coaching: From the Leader to the Team to the Company"

Marshall Goldsmith
The Art and Practice of Leadership Coaching (2005)

This article provides a case study to explain the significance of coaching for helping successful leaders achieve positive change in behavior. The case study details how an executive expanded a simple coaching assignment to benefit not only his team but also the entire company. It lists learning points for coaching, including the importance of involving team members and key stakeholders.

"CEO's Ascent Was Years in the Making"

Linda Wilson
Modern Healthcare (July 2005)

This article discusses the successful succession plan at Pomona Valley Hospital Medical Center. One of the goals of its succession planning structure is to always have one or two people being developed for a higher-level leadership role.

"Florida's Martin Memorial: Growing Talent from Within"

Linda Wilson
Modern Healthcare (2005)

This article discusses Martin Memorial Health System's leadership development program and success stories of employees who were promoted from within through the program.

"Best Practices in Career Path Definition and Succession Planning"

Report-Best Practices LLC

This Best Practices Benchmarking Report examines career path definition and leadership development with the goal of enabling companies to design and implement successful career path and succession planning systems.

"Succession Planning Demystified"

W. Hirsh
IES Report 372 (2000)

This article gives a background of what succession planning is, what organizations use it for, and how they are produced. It identifies concepts such as skill development and assessment processes as important factors to incorporate into a succession plan. It also discusses how succession planning has changed to fit with modern times.

"Succession Planning: A Tool for Success"

Jana Ritter
Galt Global Review (April 2003)

This article discusses how important it is for companies to plan for resignations and retain talented employees. It offers six basic criteria for a succession plan to succeed, including ongoing commitment of high-level management. A case study is also included.

"Successful Succession Planning"

David G. Javitch
www.entrepreneur.com (June 2005)

This article discusses the difficulties in deciding who should succeed the owner of a family-owned business and offers tips on making this tough decision. It suggests giving serious consideration to prospects outside the family and explains why.

"Lesson's from McDonald's Tragedy: Always Have a Succession Plan"

Carol Hymowitz and Joann S. Lublin
www.careerjournal.com (2005)

This article discusses the importance of having a succession plan ready in the event of a sudden death of top-level executives. It uses as an example the effective succession plan McDonald's had in place when this happened to its chairman and chief executive.

"Succession Screw-ups"

Business Week (2005)

This article contrasts McDonald's effective succession planning system with the almost nonexistent one of Coca-Cola Co., and discusses the importance of having a successor ready to take over in the event of a sudden executive loss.

"Faxon Named Brandier Heir"

Susan Butler and Emmanuel Legrand
Billboard (2005)

This article discusses the succession plan of EMI Group, which involves the company's chief financial officer becoming the worldwide president/chief operating officer.

"Succession Planning: It's Not Just for Your Executive Team"

Adam Miller

www.learningcircuits.org (March 2005)

Discusses the importance of viewing succession planning that happens every day, throughout an organization, impacting every employee. It also discusses several important elements of succession planning, including detailed skill assessments and robust internal recruiting operations. Highlights the importance of career profiling and team building tools.

"Choose Tomorrow's Leaders Today"

Robert M. Fulmer

gbr.pepperdine.edu

This article illustrates findings from a study conducted by sixteen firms and the American Productivity and Quality Center that looked at the best succession management practices of large firms. It states that the best succession management practices are dynamic and change as the company changes.

"Succession Planning When There's No Apparent Heir"

Theodore P. Burbank

www.buysellbiz.com

This article covers ten steps to effective succession planning and stresses the importance of what your business requires and what your business is worth.

"ConAgra Foods Chairman Announces Succession Plan and Search for Successor"

Business Wire (May 2005)

This article covers the succession plan of ConAgra, initiated by the chief executive officer and chairman, Bruce Rohde. The plan utilizes a search committee to choose his immediate successor.

"The Strategy of Succession Planning"

M. Dana Baldwin

www.strategyletter.com (July 2001)

This article discusses succession planning as an important part of a company's strategic planning. Includes key elements to a succession plan, such as long-term direction of your company and the career paths your most talented people are following. Also outlines seven advantages of succession planning.

"Succession Planning: A Tool for Success"

Jana Ritter
Galt Global Review (April 2003)

This article cites a study of twenty-five global talent leaders who found that the engagement and retention of talent has become a mission-critical priority for sustaining leadership in the marketplace. Discusses basic criteria required for any succession plan to succeed. Also includes an interview with Watson Wyatt, president of the Personnel Department, recognized as one of the best twenty-five companies to work for.

"Succession Planning Not Just for Top Execs"

Robert K. Prescott
Human Resource Management News (June 2000)

This article discusses the importance of having a succession plan covering all levels of an organization. Discusses how employer investments in training or succession planning efforts are actually retention strategies that can preserve existing talent.

"Choosing a Successful Successor"

Carole Matthews
Inc.com (October 2001)

This article highlights key questions (and the reasoning behind these questions) important for the successful implementation of a succession plan, including, Where is the business going? And who are the stakeholders?

"To Help Others Develop, Start with Yourself"

Marshall Goldsmith
www.fastcompany.com (March 2004)

This article discusses how great leaders encourage leadership development by developing themselves and directly and actively being involved in leadership development. The article states that organizations with highly effective leaders tend to more actively manage their talent.

"Bench Strength: Grooming Your Next CEO"

Jay A. Conger and Robert M. Fulmer
Harvard Business Review (January 2004)

This article discusses the importance of combining succession planning and leadership development. It highlights benefits of action learning programs, such as providing developmental experiences for employees.

"The Art and Science of Talent Management"

Rochelle Turoff Mucha
Organization Development (March 2004)

This article discusses how businesses need to acquire a new understanding of and leverage talent differently if they are to thrive during both the best and worst of times.

"Succession Planning: Reflect on All Concerns"

I. Gregg Van Wert
American Printer (July 2004)

This article discusses family-owned businesses and the importance and significance of having a succession plan in place for when the founder leaves the business. It offers suggestions regarding easing the transition for all parties involved and making timelines.

"Succession Planning: Make Decisions Now, Alleviate Headaches"

Marc Wieder
Real Estate Weekly (June 2005)

This article discusses succession planning in relation to real estate investors. It offers specific advice and explains ways to most effectively leave the business in the hands of family members.

"Succession Planning Lags"

HR magazine (September 2004)

This article explains the importance of having a succession plan in place for senior leadership positions. It discusses the potential for more companies to involve their HR division in the succession planning process as there is some evidence that involving HR works.

"Effective Succession Planning"

Matthew Tropiano Jr.
Defense AT & L (May–June 2004)

This article explains the vital components of succession planning and includes educational training as part of the definition. Vital components explained include CEO and leadership commitment and involvement and competency models. It also gives examples of successful companies that use varied competency models.

"Succession Planning for a Privately Held Business"

Richard A. Hamm
RMA Journal (April 2004)

This article explores seven important elements of a good succession plan, focusing on privately held or family-owned businesses. These include selecting and announcing the next head of the business as early as possible and planning for governance with a board of directors that includes outsiders.

"Succession Planning: Still Broken; Why Many Companies Aren't Getting It Right"

Roger M. Kenny
Chief Executive (January–February 2004)

This article uses Boeing's Phil Condit being forced out and Motorola's hiring an outsider as CEO as examples of a general lack of good succession planning practices within companies. It discusses possible ways for companies to better utilize succession planning.

"Succession Planning and Management"

Teresa Howe, CHRP
www.charityvillage.org (January 2004)

Discusses the realities of today's talent pool, such as widespread retirements of the baby boom generation and the potential costliness of hiring externally. Also highlights the importance of implementing an organizational chart, detailing a succession management process, and measuring the effectiveness of it.

"A Buyer's Job Market: In the New War for Talent, Acquirers Want Only the Right People—At the Right Price"

Lori Calabro
CFO: Magazine for Senior Financial Executives (November 2004)

This article discusses the pros and cons of using retention bonuses to keep talented employees in a company. It discusses the significance of decisions, including which employees to give retention bonuses to and how much to pay.

"Succession Planning Is Planning for Success"

John Beeson
Kansas City Star (2005)

This article includes myths and fallacies that are causes of failures in succession planning at the chief executive officer and senior executive level, such as waiting for retirement and an overreliance on outside recruitment. It discusses how some leading corporations are incorporating periodic meetings with human resources to develop a better succession planning approach.

"Succession Planning Not Just for Big Business"

Kurt Williams
Idaho Business Review (2005)

This article discusses the importance of succession planning for small, midsized, and family-run businesses. It also gives two main reasons why there is a gap between available talent and job openings, including the fact that baby boomers will soon be entering retirement. It gives General Electric's succession planning process as an example of a successful succession planning program.

Key Elements of a Business Succession Plan"

Ward B. Anderson
Life and Health/Financial Services Edition (2005)

This article states that avoiding the issue of succession planning puts businesses at financial risk. It also explains certain issues that are common to succession planning, such as control, valuation, and funding.

"Decisions; Succession Planning; Who's Next?"

Financial Director (2005)

This article discusses the value of succession planning for making an organization more dynamic. It states that identifying and promoting top talent sends a positive message to these employees and boosts staff retention. It also suggests that talent management gives a company a better chance of retaining employees.

"Succession Management: Filling the Leadership Pipeline; Succession Management Ranks High on CEOs' Priority Lists, Yet Many Companies Have No Formal Program in Place. Here's How to Turn Talk into Action—and Competitive Advantage"

Chief Executive

This article uses the University of Pittsburgh Medical Health System as a good example of using succession planning to promote innovation within an organization. Its succession planning program provides a model for a new approach to developing leaders for the entire health care industry. The article also includes a discussion on the disconnect between what executives think about succession planning and what is put into practice.

"How To: Here Are 10 Tips on Developing a Successful Succession Program—News You Can Use"

Tracy Burns-Martin
T & D (November 2002)

This article supplies ten useful tips on succession planning, including setting the goal, designing the program, and evaluating the program.

"Help Wanted: Superhero; Most Companies Drop the Baton When It Comes to CEO Succession. Here's What a Few Do Right-Succession

Des Dearlove and Stuart Crainer
Chief Executive (2002)

This article discusses five major failings of succession plans, including no objective set of selection criteria and not looking beyond the most visible senior management candidates. Many examples of companies who have instituted successful succession planning programs are given in this article.

Software

OrgPlus

www.orgplus.com

OrgPlus allows companies to create and manipulate their own personal organizational charts. It lets companies create scenarios to plan for change and is used by more than four hundred Fortune 500 companies.

Succession Wizard

www.successionwizard.com

Allows a company to create and organize a succession plan. It includes the ability to create reports that display management planning information that can be configured to match a company's criteria.

Sapien.HCM Edition

www.sapiensoftware.com

Includes succession planning, management development, and organizational chart features to help make it easier for a company to be effective in these areas.

ETWeb

www.executrack.com

This is a Web-based software package for career and succession planning. Features include candidacies and succession scenarios as well as succession management metrics.

ProfileXT Assessment

www.assessmentspecialists.com

Software designed to reflect core competencies of current top performers in a company. It also has features that conduct a competency gap analysis.

iCareerManager

www.insala.com

Software designed to help organizations remain competitive by developing, retaining, and redeploying top talent.

eHR Pulse System

www.pilat-nai.com

Software is a Web-based ASP service. Functions include producing successor charts and comparison of employees based on competencies.

HRM Connect Executive

www.hrmsoftware.com

Software provides comprehensive support for HR planning, helping to make succession planning and talent management more effective.

Web Sites

www.SuccessFactors.com
www.successionplannings.net
www.MyWiseOwl.com
www.hrexecutiveforum.com

Videos

Retaining Top Talent

21 minutes
Lynn Ware

Mindleaders.com, Inc. (2000–2001)

Helps you identify the risks of attrition and uses the TALENT model to identify specific retention practices to retain your most valued employees. Applicable to front-line managers, mid-level managers, and executives.

Succession Planning

19 minutes
Anne Bruce
MindLeaders.com, Inc. (2000–2001)

Shows you how to eliminate panic hiring, develop a succession plan, and provide significant career guidance to employees. Applicable to front-line managers, mid-level managers, and executives.

Motivate to Retain (Interview)

21 minutes
Anne Bruce
MindLeaders.com, Inc. (2000–2001)

Anne Bruce describes how you can motivate and retain key employees. Applicable to front-line managers, mid-level managers, and executives.

Retention for the Long Haul

6 minutes
Lynn Ware
MindLeaders.com, Inc. (2000–2001)

Dr. B. Lynn Ware, industrial psychologist, discusses the trends impacting retention and what managers can do to retain key employees. Applicable to front-line managers, mid-level managers, and executives.

Conferences

Designing and Implementing Succession Management Systems

Linkage, Inc.
See www.linkageinc.com for workshop dates and locations.

Training involves learning about critical decision points and conditions for implementing an effective succession management system.

Index